God's Glory on Display

God's Glory on Display: The PLAY BOOK
Copyright © 2022 Mary A. Baker

All rights reserved.

No part of this publication may be reproduced in a retrieval system, or transmitted in any form or by any means—electronic, mechanical, photocopying, recording, or otherwise—without the prior written permission of the publisher.

Unless otherwise noted, scriptures taken from the Holy Bible, New International Version®, NIV®. Copyright © 1973, 1978, 1984, 2011 by Biblica, Inc.™ Used by permission of Zondervan. All rights reserved worldwide. www.zondervan.com The "NIV" and "New International Version" are trademarks registered in the United States Patent and Trademark Office by Biblica, Inc.™ Scripture quotations marked TPT are from The Passion Translation®. Copyright © 2017, 2018 by Passion & Fire Ministries, Inc. Used by permission. All rights reserved. ThePassionTranslation.com. The Holy Bible, English Standard Version® (ESV®) Copyright © 2001 by Crossway, a publishing ministry of Good News Publishers. All rights reserved. ESV Text Edition: 2016.

This manuscript has undergone viable editorial work and proofreading, yet human limitations may have resulted in minor grammatical or syntax-related errors remaining in the finished book. The understanding of the reader is requested in these cases. While precaution has been taken in the preparation of this book, the publisher and author assume no responsibility for errors or omissions, or for damages resulting from the use of the information contained herein.

This book is set in the typeface *Athelas* designed by Veronika Burian and Jose Scaglione.

Paperback (compact) ISBN: 978-1-955546-18-8
Paperback (full size) ISBN: 978-1-955546-29-4
Hardcover ISBN: 978-1-955546-30-0

Published in Partnership with *Tall Pine Books*
119 E Center Street, Suite B4A | Warsaw, Indiana 46580
www.tallpinebooks.com

| 1 22 22 20 16 02 |

Published in the United States of America

God's Glory on

The PLAY BOOK

Mary A. Baker

"Everything changed for me back in the winter of 2009. I had come to a place of utter desperation - financially, personally, spiritually and creatively - where all my options seemed to disappear. It was in that moment, God drew me into a season of intentional worship and prayer to soak in His presence. This ended up lasting for about 2 months. During that season, God recalibrated my heart, healed old wounds that had been dominating my life for years and set me on a course in His Kingdom that I'm still following today as both an artist and entrepreneur. It was in His presence that I was transformed forever.

In her book, God's Glory on Display, my friend Mary Baker dives deep into that same transformative power I experienced that's available to all believers in God's presence. Out of her own journey of encountering the Lord over many years, Mary shares practical insights and strategies that make it simple for any believer to encounter Jesus in a more authentic way. I highly recommend this book and the work Mary is doing to enable people to be transformed by the presence of God."

–Matt Tommey
Artist, Author & Mentor
www.MattTommeyMentoring.com

"The title of this book carries more power and weight than mere words can communicate. The wide-eyed wonder and childlike simplicity of vivid encounters with God was evident to me as I sat with Mary Baker on a river's edge; our feet immersed in the cold waters of a spring in Colorado. As the water rushed past us, she giggled. I turned to look at her, noticing that her eyes were like beams of light and her smile radiated a joy beyond the seen realm. I inquired about why she laughed. Her reply took me into a special place: "I just saw a huge red heart coming down the river from the throne." We pondered the presence and the gifts of God that flow to us daily, and we were reminded to be aware to catch them in the river of gladness. This is how Mary Baker lives each day, and I am beyond delighted that she has written God's Glory on Display (The Play Book), because I know that my time with her on the river's edge will become a doorway for thousands of people to behold the unseen and live in childlike awe of our Father. "

–Traci Vanderbush
Minister & Author
www.tracivanderbush.com

"This book does not have my endorsement because Mary Baker is my friend, a gifted speaker, a strong woman after God's own heart, and carries an authentic prophetic grace. While all those things are true, God's Glory on Display has my whole hearted endorsement because the body of Christ needs this book! Mary Baker has experienced some things that are supernatural on a biblical level. And these mind blowing encounters with the miracle working power of God have produced in her the humility of a student rather than the pride of an expert. The fruit of learning from humble teachers is confidence in the knowledge that God will do the same through you. If you will welcome the process, this book will challenge you in the best way, but also might just step on your toes. That's not a bad thing. The practical Holy Spirit infused wisdom in Mary's generous supply of experiences will dissolve areas where you feel spiritually stuck. It also confronts an ignorance and immaturity all too often on display in people who are called to ministry, and then martyr their reputations at the hand of their own zeal and call it persecution. That's just one of many reasons the church desperately needs this book and Mary Baker's voice. God's Glory on Display can keep you from shipwrecking your own ministry if you will learn from it. If you are a Pastor, prayer leader, healing minister, or teacher, you owe it to the body of Christ to get this book into the hands of your congregation, students, and ministry team."

–BILL VANDERBUSH
Author/Speaker, *Faith Mountain Ministries*

"Intimacy with God has too often been mixed with the religious trappings of spiritual striving and self-abasement. Mary is a prophetic psalmist who masterfully unfolds the secret depths of God's presence from a place of oneness and divine union that honors the work of Christ, and makes the glory realms accessible to all of us. The accompaniment tracks on the website are the perfect assistant for drowning out distractions, creating atmospheres of encounter, and ushering us in to an awareness of God's presence."

–DAN MCCOLLAM
Author, speaker, and co-founder
of *Bethel School of the Prophets*
www.propheticcompany.com

"Jim and Mary Baker have been personal friends for years. One of the things I love about the author of *God's Glory on Display* is her passionate pursuit of the glorious outpouring of the Holy Spirit that is currently taking place. My life has been transformed as I have had encounters that led me to a process. In *God's Glory on Display*, you'll receive revelation, impartation, and activation into the unseen realm so you can see the invisible and do the impossible. Say "Yes" to the process! Mary can be trusted as a guide and the Holy Spirit will rest on you as you surrender to His love."

–Leif Hetland
President, *Global Mission Awareness*,
Author, *The Love Awakening*

"Perhaps you have longed to have a deeper relationship with the Father the way the prophets did. Through her own personal experiences, Mary Baker shares with us how that can become a reality in our own lives. Not only does she lead you into encounters with the Father, but she has included short audio clips that will enhance your journey into greater intimacy with the three in one. As Mary would say, you will find yourself being immersed in His womb where all dreams and transformation begin. Isn't this what we all long for? Why not let Mary show you how!"

—Brian and Candice Simmons
Passion and Fire Ministries

CONTENTS

Foreword xi
Preface xiii

1. A REVELATION OF ONENESS 1
   Revelatory Encounter 1 13

2. UNTETHERED 17
   Revelatory Encounter 2 19

3. GOD'S GLORY ON DISPLAY 23
   Revelatory Encounter 3 33

4. DELIGHTING EFFECTS 37
   Revelatory Encounter 4 49

5. THE REALITY OF ONENESS 53
   Revelatory Encounter 5 65

6. THE FULLNESS 71
   Revelatory Encounter 6 85

7. TRAPDOORS 89
   Revelatory Encounter 7 103

8. SET APART 107
   Revelatory Encounter 8 117

9. KISS & TELL 121
   Revelatory Encounter 9 129

10. PRIESTLY KINGS AND KINGLY PRIESTS 135
    Revelatory Encounter 10 145

11. THE LIVING WATER 151
    Revelatory Encounter 11 161

    Meet the Author 165

FOREWORD

Every person who has made an impact on history for the Lord has had one thing in common: they had an encounter with God.

In fact, it was a lifestyle of encountering God.

As someone once said, if information was all we needed we'd all be skinny, rich, and happy. People don't need more information; they need transformation.

One of the main ways Christians are transformed is through encounter. We encounter Jesus through His word, His presence, His truth, His voice, in worship, spiritual disciplines, depending on Him for strength, and in countless other ways.

The Christian life was never meant to be a set of religious doctrines we believe or pious practices we routinely follow. We are not to be known for our discipline; we are to be known for our passion. It is about a living, interactive relationship with a Person.

Maybe you've never thought of this, but Christianity was never meant to just have one encounter at salvation. Peter was filled with the Spirit in the upper room when Jesus breathed on him and the other disciples (John 20:22), on the day of Pentecost (Acts 2:4), and subsequently two more times in the book of Acts (Acts 4:8, 31.) The apostle Paul was filled with the Spirit on three separate occasions in Acts (9:17; 13:9, 52).

In fact, Paul, commands believers to "be filled continually with the Holy Spirit" (Ephesians 5:18 TPT). It is staying connected to His presence and voice that allows us to pray prayers and live lives that shape the course of history.

The greatest privilege known to humanity is to know God by experience. And this is why *God's Glory on Display* is such a gift.

Mary has given us a guidebook to lead you into your own encounters with God. She has a gift for making the mystical parts of the Bible accessible and the experiential side of our relationship with Him less "weird."

This is not a book of theory for her. Having been married to her for 28 years, this is her lifestyle. She is uniquely gifted for this.

So set aside some unhurried time, read the book, and be led into an encounter with Jesus.

You were born for this.

–JIM BAKER
Senior Leader of *Zion Christian Fellowship*
Founder of *WealthWithGod.com*

PREFACE

I love creating a space for people to meet the Lord in a new and real way. Not just creating a space, but my favorite thing is when, out of this space, someone gets a new revelation, guidance, or an answer from God that transforms their thought patterns and outward expression so that they realize how good God really is and how *for them* He really is.

Sometimes the smallest revelation can bring about the biggest changes. And these revelations from a simple encounter with God uncover the real you that heaven is cheering on to become a great and powerful display of God's glory.

Many books I have read are full of great information, and my knowledge grows, but there is usually no invitation at the end of each chapter to really talk about it with the Lord, ask Him about it, and *see for myself*. So, let's follow the Scripture's permission to encounter God like never before.

Here are a few Scriptures to encourage you in this permission:

In the morning, LORD, You hear my voice; in the morning I lay my requests before You and wait expectantly. (Psalm 5:3)

Ask, and it will be given to you; seek, and you will find; knock, and it will be opened to you. For everyone who asks receives, and the one who seeks finds, and to the one who knocks it will be opened. Or which one of you, if his son asks him for bread, will give him a stone? Or if he asks for a fish, will give him a serpent? If you then, who are evil, know how to give good gifts to your children, how much more will your Father who is in heaven give good things to those who ask him! (Matthew 7:7-11)

Therefore I tell you, whatever you ask in prayer, believe that you have received it, and it will be yours. (Mark 11:24)

Until now you have asked nothing in my name. Ask, and you will receive, that your joy may be full. (John 16:24 NKJV)

My hope in creating this book is that it will be a see-for-yourself kind of book; that you will not just read something new, take my word for it, and walk away, but actually have an experience with the Three in One, the Lord Himself, so that you can continue to become transformed inside and out. This book is about getting a revelation of your oneness with the Creator and what it looks like to live as God's glory on display.

But as for me, I will continue to gaze upon your face—until I see you for Who you really are.

As I discover what pleases You, then I will awaken with Your form and be fully satisfied.

Fulfilled in the revelation of Your glory in me! (Psalm 17:15 TPT)

That One Encounter

Remember the Saul-to-Paul conversion in Acts 9? In short, a light shone around Saul. He heard the voice of Jesus and was blinded. God sent a prophet to remove the scales from his eyes so that he could see again, and then the prophet told Paul how he was going to be God's instrument in winning a massive number of Gentiles to the Lord. That ONE ENCOUNTER changed everything that day for Saul, including his name.

See, Saul (before he became Paul) knew all of the traditions, feasts, and laws of the Bible and was very passionate about keeping them. But without the encounter or experience of Jesus' voice, who was the fulfillment of the law, the Bible was just a bunch of rules to be kept and feasts to attend. And to top it off, he was completely out of the will of the Lord by persecuting Christians. He was actually living the exact opposite of his calling in life. Eek!

The Jews without Jesus totally missed the punchline. Jesus IS the Word and the fulfillment of the law, and the reason the feasts were a thing was all making way for the Messiah, Jesus.

When our knowledge increases, so should our experience of God's power and voice. So, as you carry on through this book, stay in a teachable place with the Lord, and let Him guide you into Him and His Truth, not just mine. Do not try to read all the chapters at once, but maybe try to read one a week or one a day. Take your time and slow down with the Lord.

My hope is that as you draw nearer to the Lord throughout every encounter, you will be so transformed that you cannot help but have a deeper revelation of your oneness with the Three in One—moving like He does (in power and authority), talking like He does (with kindness and gentleness), loving like He does (without conditions), and lastly, being filled with joy overflowing!

Let's party!

–Mary

I

A REVELATION OF ONENESS

Your crucifixion with Christ has severed the tie to this life, and now your true life is hidden away <u>in God in Christ.</u> And as Christ himself is seen for who he really is, who you really are will also be revealed, for you are now <u>one with him in his glory</u>! (Colossians 3:3 TPT, emphasis added)

We must have a revelation of our oneness to display God's glory and display it in a way that reflects Him well.

There is a journey to deepening the revelation of true oneness that is set before each follower of Christ and everyone has a choice to enter into it. I have been on this journey, and this journey will never end, as we will never run out of new truths and places to uncover about God–*if* we want to know them.

Your true life is hidden in Christ. It's a mystery. You won't comprehend with your brain first, but only by surrendering to Truth Himself and allowing Holy Spirit to reveal it.

One of my largest pit-stops on this journey was when one of our guest speakers gave me a prophetic word about how God was going to take me into the "inner-inner chambers." Little did I know that seeking the meaning behind this word would change my life forever.

It was one of those times when my spirit was receiving this word, but my brain was like, "Does-not-compute."

After mulling over the word again the next day, I asked God, "Is there such a place as the inner-inner chambers or is this word a little 'off'?"

Side note: If you are wired like me at all and love seeking out the mystical places of the Lord, we have to be extra careful not to go exploring just anywhere in the spirit realm. We must always be grounded in the Word (the Bible) and go where HE wants to take us. Otherwise, we start losing our grounding in the Lord and seek a false power source without even knowing it. Some people have an experience, revelation, or encounter with the Lord through visions, dreams, and His voice—and *then* go to Scripture to make sure it's legit. Others are wired the opposite: they need to first get the revelation from Scripture and *then* other things like visions, angels, dreams, etc. will follow. Of course, Holy Spirit can shatter any of our wirings and do whatever He wants! But those are typically the two ways it goes with people, and I am wired the first way I mentioned.

Back to the story. I started seeking the Lord about this word I got from this trusted source and began searching the Scriptures to back up the word. Sure enough, I found something. Praise Him!

Draw me into your heart. We will run away together into the <u>king's chamber inside of a chamber</u>. (Song of Songs 1:4 TPT, emphasis added)

I was relieved and excited. Now I had a grounding. I was still a little troubled, though, because I wasn't sure how to get to this place, spiritually. I would seek God in my alone time with Him and did not get anywhere new. It was about time for a personal retreat, so off I went for the sole purpose of getting to this place with the Lord!

Within a two-hour drive, I was surrounded by a wintery lake and forest at a lodge in Ohio. I had a room with an incredible view of God's creation. Every morning, I would wake up and ask the Lord to take me into the inner-inner chambers. And every morning for the next three days—He was silent.

For three days.

I did the only thing I knew to do: delight in Him. Worship Him. Not to *get* something from Him but just to *be* with Him and have fun with Him; commune with Him, talk and listen, praise and thank Him for what He has done and what He will do. It is my joy to come before the throne of God like a child and love on Him unconditionally.

When we see His hand at work, yes, that provokes something in us to shout "THANK YOU, JESUS!" But there are also those times when it is simply our privilege and delight to do it. I am wowed by His love for me and His hand on my life. I am wowed by His majesty and beauty. I am wowed by His kindness and mercy. I am wowed by the gifts He gives freely. I am wowed by His ability to wipe every slate clean.

I am just wowed by God. There really is no one else I'd rather be with all the time than Him. (Don't worry, I love being with my family and people, as well.) It is such a glorious time when you can just *be* with the Lord with no other agenda except the one He wants to make.

Once we learn how to die to our own agenda with God or what we think He owes us in a certain time slot, delighting in Him kicks in. That's when the true relationship deepens and you are able to draw from the Living Water flowing from your belly. Those are joy-filled times!

On the fourth day, He finally told me, "Close your eyes, Mary."

I often close my eyes to drown out distractions when I am with the Lord and ask Him to take me where He wants. This is using your sanctified imagination. There is a difference than just making stuff up in your head. The more you are with Him and in Scripture, the more you will understand the difference. The Holy Spirit guides your thoughts and scenery in your mind. When you presented your body as a living sacrifice, you presented everything—including your imagination. The sanctified imagination becomes the canvas that Holy Spirit can paint on because our human language is limited and cannot always depict what God reveals in an accurate way.

As I began to enter the Lord's reality, I was expecting to go to someplace in heaven or in the universe or something. But I didn't. Instead, I found myself standing in what I can only describe as the womb of Christ. I had a *knowing* that I was in the womb of Christ.

I began weeping as the revelation of unity with Christ was gently but forcefully engulfing my entire being. I still can't really put it into words. It was an understanding of our complete unification with Him that was downloaded in an instant, sort of like *The Matrix* movie.

The Lord then told me to open my eyes. I did.

And as I looked out my window, guess what I saw.

The exact same thing I saw before I closed my eyes: a lake, trees, birds, snow. I was back in my reality—only this time, I was seeing everything AS Jesus, like my eyes were His eyes. It was a little freaky at first. Being *that* one with someone as if my body was seized by someone else.

First John 4:17 says, "As Christ is so are you in this world."

Meaning, we ACT AS CHRIST, and we MOVE AS CHRIST. This became a very real Scripture to me at this moment.

I was so thrown back, though, because everything looked NATURAL and I was expecting MYSTICAL.

The lake I was looking at...normal.

The landscape, the snow...normal.

The only difference was, I was not alone! I was

VERY AWARE that Jesus was WATCHING ALL OF THIS THROUGH MY EYES and my eyes through His. It was like He was window gazing through me.

Talk about "search me, oh God." I felt naked because I was very aware He knew and could see EVERYTHING that was in me.

At that moment, nothing was hidden.

I was definitely taken to a new place—a very intimate place. And to my surprise, I got a new revelation of oneness with the Lord.

Because this moment along my journey has impacted my life so much, I am writing this book in hopes of helping bring you into your own moment, your own encounters, and your own revelation of just how ONE you are with the God of the universe.

Only Jesus becoming real to you will change you in such a way that there is no more wrestling between living like the world and living like children of the King. When we allow ourselves to come into Him at a deeper level, an unhindered level, we can see things we have never seen before in the natural and the spiritual. We can do things we have never done before because faith has galloped over hope. It's great to have hope, but when faith kicks in, it brings what you had been hoping for to an actual manifestation of heaven on earth.

"God can speak any way He wants to!" —Bobby Conner

We must be open to any way God wants to speak to us. Maybe you will not have an encounter like mine for

Him to give you a revelation of our oneness. It could be as simple as a whisper in your ear from the Holy Spirit. But pay attention because He is always speaking.

Call to me and I will answer you and tell you great and unsearchable things you do not know. (Jeremiah 33:3)

God's desire is to shatter our limiting beliefs. He is God and He wants to reveal different aspects of Himself to us that will blow our minds sometimes. He is so complex, yet so simple. He uses our simple, human/earthly knowledge to communicate the complexity of Himself. We just need to be willing to open our spiritual eyes to go there, like standing in His womb.

I asked Blake Healey about metaphoric things that happen in the spirit realm and he explained it like this:

Your apps on your phone are metaphors. When you click on it, it zooms in, but it's not physically zooming in, it's just a metaphor. What is actually happening is a bunch of zeros and ones. So, what is actually happening is almost incomprehensible to most people, so we create a series of metaphors on every computer so that we can actually interact with it. It's not a perfect comparison but it's the same kind of thing in that there is no magic thing happening when you lay your hands on someone—it does not create a circuit literally, but it is like windows for the spirit. The difference is that we connect to something that is real.

Along those same lines of shattering our limiting beliefs, in the Womb Encounter I told you about, I was only expecting the "mystical manifestations," like a cloud of smoke, a swirling cloud of gold specs, gold dust, oil, gold teeth, outer space, etc. because that is what I had only *heard of* or experienced. This encounter was not as much "mystical" as it was Him showing me how natural the supernatural can be—especially when we use it in this earthly realm.

We must not limit how God speaks to us. God speaks to us in the language we will "get it" in. And because when God speaks, things continue to be created forever, there will be layers of us "getting it."

Some of you may be thinking, "I disagree. He talks to me in symbols all the time and I have no idea what they mean!" It is His desire that you journey with Him and *ask* Him what they mean or what He is trying to tell you. As you search for the answer, it draws you closer to Him because you are doing it *with* Him.

> *It is the glory of God to conceal a matter, But the glory of kings is to search out a matter. (Proverbs 25:2 NASB)*

And also, it is the way He created you. You may think you cannot understand because you don't believe you are capable of thinking in this manner, but as you start owning the version of you that heaven sees, you will be able to flow with the Holy Spirit to reveal all that He has hidden for you to find. It is ALL in Christ, which is in you.

Sometimes, we keep our identity and origin in the earth—but you were created by the Maker and reborn into and from a spirit realm when you accepted and decided to follow Jesus Christ. You are now an alien to earth. Identify with that.

Beloved, I urge you as aliens and strangers to abstain from fleshly lusts which wage war against the soul. (1 Peter 2:11)

I have a friend, Reece Saunders, who said a phrase once that I live my life by: *"Not everything means **something**, but **some things** mean more than you think."*

I am the person (as I am sure many of you are, too) who sees a wild animal while driving and asks the Lord if He's speaking to me through it. Or while talking to the Lord about something and needing direction, I will see the answer on a billboard or a license plate or a hawk will fly across my front windshield.

God is ALWAYS speaking. We just have to pay attention to find out how. It's like a treasure hunt!

The Womb of His Desire

When we have encounters, sometimes it's a good idea to have other prophets or trusted people around you to help you judge if things are from God or not—especially when they are so weird.

I was visiting with one of our friends who is a prophet and I was asking him about my Womb Encounter.

He told me, "Mary, you are one with Jesus and when

you minister, He outshines you. Kathryn Kuhlman—she didn't *try* to do miracles. It was out of revelation that she is one with the Spirit. She would pray, '**What is the womb of Your desire, Lord?**' before her meetings."

Can I just say, I was so relieved to hear he didn't think I was a crazy person after sharing my Womb Encounter?! Better yet, he confirmed that this was truly from the Lord. Whew! To top it off, Kathryn Kuhlman, a respected Revivalist, used the word "womb"!

Access to miracles and access to God's desires that He would like to birth, simply come from living your life out of your revelation of oneness.

What is the "Womb"?

I thought maybe some of you had a burning question I should try to answer: What is the womb?

Well, I am not sure there is one answer to this, but I will give you what I've got.

I believe the womb is the innermost being. It is the innermost place where life is born through intimacy unveiled, love, desire, and passion that connect in a way that causes God's dreams to be seeded and then realized.

As we water the seed by communing with and through Holy Spirit, the dream seed grows and forms. As we keep honoring the Holy Spirit and the dreams of God, the seed matures into something with shape, endurance, beauty, and purpose.

The womb of Jesus is an incubator of His dreams and your dreams becoming one—intertwining, growing, and developing. Each moment you spend in the womb, the most intimate place, the quicker and more established heaven's plans manifest on earth.

Because the more real that realm is to you, the more you believe. Faith becomes unquestionable. Revelation, knowledge, and understanding grow in that realm, as well. The stronger that faith, the more growth in the things of the Spirit, and the more time you spend there—the more you are aware of Him here in the earthly realm during your daily chores of life.

As this happens, your oneness is moving as it should. Heaven is colliding with earth. You realize the moment you move as one because you now notice Jesus is peering through those eyes of yours. His hands are moving with your hands. His mouth, your mouth. What you see, He sees. He is no longer distant to you, but right inside of you, and you feel like you have been taken over, but you are in control of yielding or not.

How many times do we pray to Him and our habit is to look toward heaven or close our eyes and think of Him in heaven? He is in heaven, but He is also in you. If you want to really be freaked out today, ponder this thought: Heaven is inside of you because Holy Spirit is inside of you. What?!

We carry heaven because we carry God's very Spirit. My point is, that as you begin to realize more and more that He is peering through your eyes, you will start to pray with a little different angle. He is not distant. And

I know we *know* that and we *say* that, but I don't know many who actually pray like that.

As this awareness of Him peering through your eyes increases, you realize the complete access and Jesus' complete desire for the hurting or broken person standing right in front of you at all times. You know what you should do.

Doesn't this sound like a life worth living now? Once you've been with Him, inside His revelation heart, the drawing will never stop. You are ruined forever. (In a good way.)

We must never ignore the drawing of the Holy Spirit into intimacy but should always honor it. The more we honor what He wants to do in the room or situation we are in, the more we know how He wants to move and the more people can be set free to meet Jesus.

The less we honor Holy Spirit by ignoring His promptings, our heart gets hard of hearing and becomes sick, if you know what I mean. Dulled. Heartsick for your true love. This way of living does not bring much, if any, light to your path, let alone joy.

So, let's see where Holy Spirit is right now, and what He wants to do in this next Revelatory Encounter. Let's create space to have your own inner-inner chambers revelation.

REVELATORY ENCOUNTER 1

Listen to my walk-through of this encounter at:
www.GloryOnDisplay.com

Set aside 15-25 minutes to encounter God in a fresh way that will bring you into a deeper revelation, understanding, and reality of oneness with Him. You cannot rush this.

Have your journal ready to write down everything you see and hear (or you can write it here on this page) so that you will remember and be a good steward.

> *This is how one should regard us, as servants of Christ <u>and stewards of the mysteries of God.</u> (1 Corinthians 4:1ESV, emphasis added)*

Let's open up heaven over you, through you, and around you by praising Jesus and thanking Him for who He is and what He has done. Praying in tongues, your heavenly language, is a great idea to bring your mind and atmosphere into alignment with the Lord, as well. Pray in the Spirit for five minutes if you can.

If you have not received this gift of spiritual tongues and would like to learn how to, I would recommend going to AWMI.net and searching for "Speaking in Tongues."

Becoming Aware of God's Holy Spirit

In this moment, start to recognize that God's very Spirit is in you and hovering around you. Holy Spirit is real and ready to lead you into all things Jesus.

After you read and partner with the prayer below (or pray your own prayer, if you want), close your eyes and let Holy Spirit guide your head and heart, allowing Him to show you the King's inner-inner chamber. He may give you a different picture than the womb, so just be open. You are His unique child, and He speaks to you in your own unique way.

> *God decided in advance to adopt us into His own family by bringing us to Himself through Jesus Christ. This is what He wanted to do, and it gave Him great pleasure. (Ephesians 1:5 ESV)*

Prayer to Partner with:

Holy Spirit, I ask You to lead the way. I open up the gates of my heart to receive Your revelation of the reality of oneness with You. Would You meet me here? I lay down what I think I know and as I yield to You, open the eyes of my heart and take me to the chamber inside the King's chamber; the most intimate chamber. Lord, take me into the revelation of what our union looks like, tastes like, smells like—whatever revelation You want me to know. I'm ready and I'm listening. And Lord, correct any wrong thinking I might have along the way, as well.

Write down everything you see and hear as He takes you into the deeper places of His inner-inner chamber. What is the revelation you are receiving of how ONE you are with the Lord?

What to Expect After the Encounter:

God will cause a reviving to come to your spirit-man. This will be a personal time of resurrection where God will cause you to re-evaluate and calculate some things. Also, in things that did not make sense before, revelation and understanding will come to you. Don't forget to write it down.

2

UNTETHERED

Intimacy with the Three in One, the Godhead. I cannot go any further in this read with anything other than intimacy. God is always drawing you to Himself. He would not have sent His very own Spirit to come to dwell in you and talk to you if He didn't. The love of the Father is so deep for you. Will we ever fully grasp it on this side of heaven?

God longs to tell you the desires of His heart—His secrets, thoughts… He longs to be your friend before you ever ask Him to do anything for you.

Sometimes we skip that part, though. We forget to just enjoy Him, delight in the Lord, and be His friend because we are in a hurry or we just need Him to come through for us in an urgent situation.

But the truth is, nothing else really matters in light of His face. We live in a temporary world.

If we can get that, everything is not such an emergency anymore.

He wants us to live untethered from the earth. Not

that you don't walk out your missions, callings, and love people, and bring them to Jesus while you are on the planet. But there is a higher scope we need to operate out of: heaven. Heaven is inside us because Jesus is inside of us. We try to pull heaven down, but really it is just another reality. Not necessarily above our heads, although it could be. Another thought is, maybe it just needs to come *out*.

The Lord showed me a vision once of people hanging in mid-air, between "heaven" and earth. They were reaching so desperately for God, but they just fell short because tied around their ankle was a leather strap. One person's leather strap was tethered to their car. Another person, their house. Another, their family. Another, their job. People were grounded to the wrong things. We live in an upside-down Kingdom. This means we should be tethered to the Lord, not to the things that are not going to last. Those temporary things people were tethered to were very important to them. So important, they were made more important than God Himself, and therefore, keeping them from reaching the fullness of God. All the people had to do was cut the tether, but they were not willing.

If you have this book in your hand and you have already read this far, I know you are willing. So let's go into our next *REVELATORY ENCOUNTER* of untethering from things that might limit us so that we can move freely with the Lord for the rest of this journey.

REVELATORY ENCOUNTER 2

Listen to my walk-through of this encounter at:
www.GloryOnDisplay.com

Have your journal ready to write down everything you see and hear so that you will remember and be a good steward. (Or you can write it here on this page). Set aside 15-25 minutes for this.

Quiet yourself before the Lord. Let go of every other thought until you are left only with the thought and picture of the Lord.

If you are having a hard time focusing because of all the different thoughts in your mind, I want you to picture a door in your mind. Let's call the door, "Place Holder." Open the door and round up all of your thoughts and put them in that room, then shut the door. Tight.

Now...it's just you and Jesus, Holy Spirit, and Father God.

Lord, please silence every other voice but Yours. I give You complete control to tell me what You want to tell me, show me what You want to show me, and take me where You want to take me.

Ask Holy Spirit These Questions:

*And if you have never heard the Lord speak to you, it will often sound like your own voice in your head, only much truer and wiser.

> *Lord, show me, what am I tethered to on this planet? What temporary things have I bonded to that are holding me back or taking Your place and keeping You at arm's length? (Close your eyes to drown out distractions and allow Him to show you. After He flashes a picture or a word in your mind, write it down; it could be multiple things.)*

_____

_____

_____

_____

_____

_____

Prayer to Partner with:

> *Lord, I repent of (or turn away from) tying myself to things on this temporary planet. All I have is Yours and all You have is mine. I give You back control of every piece of my life so that I have nothing holding me back from touching You, hearing You, and making You #1 in all areas.*

Lord, would You help me be untied from the things on the earth that I made more important than You? (Allow the Lord to show you a picture of how He is untethering you from these things. Write down what you see Him do.)

_____

_____

_____

_____

_____

_____

Prayer to Partner with:

I am bound to You only, Holy Spirit! Would You come and fill those places that are freed up and empty now? (Now, allow the Holy Spirit to come inside and fill those places that are empty and scarred. Write down your experience.)

What to Expect Afterwards

You should expect to feel a freedom and joy come on you and stress lift from you. There should be a lightness in your step. You are no longer bound by the things from "Stuff Mart". You are bound by God and His burden is light.

Once we are freed from something or have an encounter with the Lord, we must always walk out what just happened. That means we don't slip back into old habits and end up putting ourselves in chains all over again.

So, from this encounter on, always walk forward and check in with Holy Spirit to see if you are walking in the same direction as Him. If you are not, ask Him to help you adjust your steps, your time, and your decisions.

3

GOD'S GLORY ON DISPLAY

What do you think of when you hear the word "glory"? When we talk about glory, we often already have an idea of what that is, based on our experience or what someone told us.

Today, we open the door for you to see and experience glory, maybe in a new light or even just a realignment. Understanding this piece about God's glory on display has everything to do with you and how you spend your days living on this planet, operating in your sphere of influence, relating to your family, excelling in your business, job, relationships...everything!

Like *some* of you, I have always felt a pull to the glory of the Lord, even though I could not quite explain what the glory of the Lord was. Anytime a speaker would come into our church and mention the word "glory," my spirit-man would jump in excitement.

There were times in a service or at home, I would moan on the ground with my face on the carpet and sometimes vibrate because what I was feeling on the inside was manifesting on the outside. I could not hold Him in. It was like I was birthing something.

It reminds me of the Song of Songs 8:5 in The Passion Translation:

I awakened your innermost being with the travail of birth as you longed for more of Me.

This deep, deep desire to be more enveloped by the glory of the Lord...it felt unquenchable. I would pray, "Lord, add the weight of Your glory to me."

My friend even had a dream one time that the Lion (Jesus) entered her house and at one point jumped on top of me and roared in my face. I just kept saying, "More weight, Lord, more weight." Normal people would want a giant, scary lion to release them, but even in dreams, He knows us and our desires.

The glory was a great mystery to me. I did not know what it really was, but I just had to know more and be in it; whatever "it" was, I was drawn to it.

For many years, I chased it.

I would see GOLD DUST raining in powerful meetings or landing on people at church. *Was that God's glory?* I would think to myself.

I would hear of a CLOUD coming in a room while people were simply worshiping God. *Was that God's glory?*

I heard of GOLD TEETH appearing in people's mouths. *Is that God's glory?*

I've seen TUMORS DISSOLVE before my eyes and miraculous healings. *Was that God's glory?*

I read many books that talked about God's glory, researching and researching. To my utter disappointment, every book I read said something totally different from the others. *Can someone just give me a straight answer, here?* Although this frustrated me, something in me knew I *needed* this glory, and I needed to understand it so that I could be all that God has called me to be and do. I was just so hungry to come into the fullness of God's glory, even though I did not have the understanding of it.

Anytime my mind was turned toward the Lord, I would feel like I was IN God's glory. But I also still felt like there was always more God wanted to show me about it; like an itch you just couldn't satisfy.

Some of you may be like, "Mary, you DON'T NEED TO UNDERSTAND everything about God—He is a MYSTERY."

And I agree with some of that. He is a mystery. But 1 Corinthians 2:9-12 says that because we have the Holy Spirit, God's mysteries are revealed to us.

I could *feel* and *recognize* glory when it came into the room, so why didn't I know what it was? I knew, but I didn't know.

It's like knowing God; you know Him, but there is a deeper knowing available.

You know ABOUT Him from what you have heard or read, but you know Him intimately when you SPEND TIME with Him and experience Him. That's where you learn of His goodness, grace, mercy, love, character, guidance, will, desires, etc.

You can know a little something ABOUT something, but you WON'T TRULY KNOW something until you experience it for yourself.

What is the Glory?

The Lord is so good to us and leaves us clues along the way when we are seeking Him and His truths. There were many clues and revelations through Scripture along this particular journey of mine. And the journey is NOT OVER, but I have at least left the garage.

I want to share a couple of Scriptures in the Bible that you may be familiar with that talk about God's glory covering the earth.

> *And blessed be His glorious name forever;*
> *And may the whole earth be filled with His glory.*
> *Amen, and Amen. (Psalm 72:19 NASB)*

> *And one called out to another and said,*
> *"Holy, Holy, Holy, is the Lord of hosts,*
> *The whole earth is full of His glory." (Isaiah 6:3 KJV)*

> *"Can a man hide himself in hiding places*
> *So I do not see him?" declares the Lord.*
> *"Do I not fill the heavens and the earth?" declares the Lord. (Jeremiah 23:24 ESV)*

So, what is the glory? Simply put, in one word, it's God. He fills the heavens and the earth. He fills all of creation, which covers the earth and speaks of who He is.

There are MANY layers to what God's glory is (this is why those glory books I read all said something different), but I just want to scratch the surface of the top three briefly before we go into a revelatory encounter time.

Firstly, God's glory is His presence. He is called "I AM" because He is whatever manifestation of His presence you need for the situation at hand. "HE IS" whatever you need Him to be in that moment. His presence COVERS it all.

In His presence is the absolute FULLNESS of joy, healing, courage, signs and wonders, and the seven-fold Holy Spirit (wisdom, revelation, understanding, knowledge, fear of the Lord, might, the Spirit of the Lord). Whatever you need in a moment, *I AM* manifests according to your faith.

His presence is like smoke that fills up every gap and crevice when you ask Him to. He saturates every part of your life that you allow Him to.

Secondly, God's glory is His goodness. Let's read Exodus 33 where Moses is talking to God about going with them as they leave Mount Sinai.

> *And he (Moses) said to him (God), "If your presence will not go with me, do not bring us up from here. For how shall it be known that I have found favor in your sight, I and your people? Is it not in your going*

> *with us, so that we are distinct, I and your people, from every other people on the face of the earth?" And the Lord said to Moses, "This very thing that you have spoken I will do, for you have found favor in my sight, and I know you by name." Moses said, "Please show me your glory." And he said, "I will make all my <u>goodness</u> pass before you and will proclaim before you my name 'The Lord.' And I will be gracious to whom I will be gracious, and will show mercy on whom I will show mercy." (Exodus 33:15-19 ESV, emphasis added)*

What makes us distinct is God's presence going with us.

In verse 19, God Himself describes His glory as His goodness. And don't you think it's strange that in the tent of meeting, back in verse 11, Moses met with the Lord face to face, and it sounded like it was a normal occurrence? Yet, Moses still asked to see God's glory?

See, His glory isn't just His presence, but it's God's very nature—His goodness. Moses wanted to go to a deeper place of *knowing* God and it was <u>found in His glory</u>. Wow.

This is intimacy with the Lord, people!

Lastly, God's glory is also Jesus.

> *The Son is the radiance of God's glory and the exact representation of his being, sustaining all things by his powerful word. (Hebrews 1:3)*

The exciting thing about this is that we are actually ONE with Jesus. THERE IS NO SEPARATION.

And because we are ONE with Jesus (who is the radiance of God's glory), His glory is inside of us. We carry it because we carry Him. He is in us and we are in Him. The deeper we go into the chambers of God's heart, the more we grow in knowing the Lord (i.e., intimacy).

As understanding and knowledge come in, HIS glory is UNVEILED TO THE WORLD: God's character, goodness, and ways. The more we KNOW HIM, the more we are able to reflect God's character and light to display Him to the world!

I Am God's Glory on Display

One day, I was at the piano and began to worship and thank the Lord. I was then led into the secret place with Him. As I worshiped, I found myself sitting at His feet. In front of me, I see Him as light spilling over on a throne.

I gazed upon His light and it was such a breathtaking display of His glorious presence. I began to sing about what I was seeing and experiencing as it was happening.

> *I come to the One*
> *Who's Holy in this place*
> *I bow right now,*
> *Your glory's on display*

It was an overwhelming sight in this place of His glory. Immediately after that, the Lord downloaded these thoughts to me and He took me into another perspective: That in the midst of storms and tragedy, I see the way through because I am a vessel (like the ark of the covenant) that carries His glory and majesty at all times. We don't just visit it, we carry it. And in these challenging times, how I respond shows people His glory.

I sang again about His glory on display, only this time, a light shone on me... The perspective was shifted as if God was singing about His glory on display, which was me. I was His glory on display. YOU are His glory on display for the world to see what He is like.

YOU are His glory that covers the earth. It's you. When you act on behalf of Jesus, you are putting God's glory on display. You are His glory on the earth.

To them God chose to make known how great among the Gentiles are the riches of the glory of this mystery, which is Christ in you, the hope of glory. (Colossians 1:27 ESV)

The mystery of the glory is, CHRIST IN YOU.

ARE YOU READY to put on a BEAUTIFUL DISPLAY of WHO GOD IS and how powerful and loving He is? Then we have to have a revelation of our oneness with Him. Not just knowing about it, but experiencing it. You won't comprehend with your brain first, but only by surrendering to Truth Himself and allowing Holy Spirit to reveal it, which we will get into in the next chapter of this book.

My heart is to help a generation move into the revelation of being so ONE with the Lord, that:

- anything is possible,
- entire cities come to know Christ because of the reflection coming off of His children, His Bride,
- there is no more sickness or disease,
- demons flee because they are no longer welcome,
- joy is in the streets,
- God's Name is famous, held in high esteem,
- His ultimate love reigns,
- and the perverted love is unable to exist.

I dream of a world where the Bride:

- no longer tries to hide her light under false, man-pleasing identities
- but MANIFESTS the FULLNESS OF CHRIST
- to BE the light and bring all men to the light, Jesus Christ, our Lord and Savior of the world.

Some of you have been feeling a battle within you that you can't explain or put words to. There has been a tug-of-war that you may be blaming on the devil, but this is actually THE UNVEILING OF CHRIST IN YOU trying to emerge from your spirit-man and manifest.

I listed my God-Mary dreams, but He has dreams inside of you, too, that have been lying in wait and forming for such a time as this. Holy Spirit wants to come out and play! He's groaning and interceding for you to come out of that cocoon and unfold those colorful wings of glory.

GOD'S GLORY WITHIN YOU WANTS TO BE ON DISPLAY. You are coming out of the cocoon, transformed into your truest identity. So let's go into the next revelatory encounter and see what God has for you today.

REVELATORY ENCOUNTER 3

Listen to my walk-through of this encounter at:
www.GloryOnDisplay.com

Find a place in your room, away from distractions (your phone, computer, projects, etc.) as you encounter the Lord for yourself. Set aside 15-25 minutes to do this.

As we go into the inner chambers with the Lord, I want to remind you that you are already in the secret place. God's very Spirit came to live inside of you and joined with your spirit when you chose to follow Jesus, so the place with Him is always right there with you to access at any time.

Now, the Bible says He is in you and you are in Him—as ONE. The question is, *how much deeper do you want to go inside*?

Will you be like Moses and ask the Lord to show you His glory? His goodness? More of who He is? Because there is always more.

I heard Bobby Conner say once, "Position yourself in a place of purity, hunger, and obedience and you will get deeper and deeper."

So, drink Him in deeply in your time with Him

today and let His life fill you up. Come to Him with a blank slate, not your own ideas.

Become aware of God's Holy Spirit, now. Any thoughts of things you have to do or take care of, lay them at His feet (you may have a picture of yourself setting these things at His feet) or simply let them lift off of you so that you are focused only on Jesus.

Start to recognize that God's very Spirit is in you and hovering around you. Holy Spirit is real and ready to lead you into all things Jesus.

Open up heaven over you, through you, and around you by praising Jesus and thanking Him for who He is and what He has done. Maybe worship Him in your spiritual language.

Let God gaze upon your heart. Realize His delight in you. As you behold Him, delight floods in.

As you are in His presence, I want you to find Him. Close your eyes and, using that sanctified imagination, allow Him to give you a picture of where He is near you.

Ask the Lord... (Write down what you see/hear)

Lord, would You show or tell me how heaven sees me? (This could be a picture, vision, words, etc.) Or who does heaven say I am?

_____
_____
_____
_____
_____

Why do You see me this way?

_____

_____

_____

_____

What else would You like to tell me about this?

_____

_____

_____

_____

Lord, what mindsets do I need to change, or what Scripture do I need to "eat" (read) in order to burst out of the cocoon and fly?

_____

_____

_____

_____

Lord, would You show or tell me what it looks like for me to be Your glory on display?

4

DELIGHTING EFFECTS

de·light | di-līt
Definition of *delight*
1: a high degree of gratification or pleasure: JOY children squealing in delight also: extreme satisfaction
2: something that gives great pleasure
3: the power of affording pleasure

Let's continue to the second part of the Song of Songs verse we read earlier, bringing us into this subject of delighting in the Lord. This is a natural flow inside the king's chamber that produces His glory.

Read it slowly with the Lord and take it in.

Draw me into your heart.
We will run away together into the
<u>king's chamber inside of a chamber</u>.
We will remember your love,
rejoicing and <u>delighting in you</u>,
celebrating your every kiss as better than wine.

No wonder righteousness adores you!
(Song of Songs 1:4 TPT, emphasis added)

When going into that inner-inner place of the Lord, in His midst is the fullness of everything. It provokes delight in us because He is so good. We cannot help but delight in God when in His chambers. He is so good, you can't ignore it.

Some might say they are "Delight Deficient." I would just say there is a delay in learning. I had this delay in learning. I might blame it on the fact that I was such an intense intercessor, and my life revolved around pleasing Him rather than enjoying Him. There was a mentor or two who would drive me to the floor on my face in prayer, because according to them and their ways, everyone had to be on their face for God to move.

I am not saying praying on your face for hours is not a good idea. I love it. But there is more. Way more. This is only one side of things. But sometimes we get so caught up in our way of learning something because we got a single revelation about it or made gold dust manifest or something.

This is where we must be careful not to get stuck on the one thing that worked but continue to expand just as God's Kingdom, goodness, and creativity are always expanding.

What if I told you manifesting God's glory (His goodness in/through you) was way easier than driving your face to the carpet in tears every day trying to pick up the burden of the Lord so that you could carry out and expand God's Kingdom on earth?

Again, not to say that being on your face is bad, but let's expand our thinking and "ways" a little more. I am not taking you out of the secret place here, only expanding what goes on within it.

Some of us can be an intense person (okay, it's me!) when in the flow of the Lord, especially when in a holy type of place, and it is okay to keep that side flowing. He is holy and intense. But things shifted for me one day. I'm not even sure when it happened but, in my secret place time with the Lord, I opened the door for Him to set the agenda instead of coming to Him with one already set.

I did this by asking "what" and "where" questions instead of "why" all the time, and amazing things happened. I asked Him questions like, "What do You want to do today? Where do You want to take me?" and a whole new world opened up to me. Not just a new world, but it was like I was in the mind and heart of Christ.

Unlike before, if I were reading a Scripture verse or had a dream that I did not understand, I would ask an opposite question of what I would normally ask. In the dream case, I used to ask "*What* does this (name) or that mean (symbolize)?" and would not hear clearly enough. So, I decided to die to the fact that I had to interpret what every symbol and scene meant in the dream. My new, more general question is, "*Why* did I have this dream?" When I changed the question, I started getting a complete download at that point.

Asking the right or different questions brings a

lot of revelation and clarity. Changing the question brought wider freedom for an answer without having to understand everything all at once. Sometimes we get caught up in having to understand everything Jesus is showing us instead of simply enjoying the answer He wants to give. And the answers He gives are always the ones we can handle and take seed inside of our spirit in order to grow and mature.

Bottom line...move and expand from only allowing intense prayer and intercession, to enjoying what the Lord wants to say and where He wants to take you today. Understanding will come along the journey. This will increase your delight in the Lord and open up your spiritual senses.

When we see Him as a some*thing*, rather than a some*one*, there is so much we miss out on. We want to know Him and His character so well that we are able to finish His sentences...like a close friend does. We already know He can finish ours! This is why we must expand from just bringing a prayer petition to actually being His friend and learning His true heart and goodness so that we can manifest the fullness of who He really is to the world.

Begin to spend more and more time letting God set the agenda instead of coming to Him with a list of things to pray about. This makes room to just sit at His feet and listen, be, and ENJOY just how good He really is. When we enjoy Him, we please Him out of that flow.

There is No Pressure

Another side effect of simply delighting or taking pleasure in the Lord is that there is no pressure. There is only a lightness that comes. Any burden you were carrying that was not of Him just floats off like a feather, which increases the pleasure of being with Him.

> *For my yoke is <u>easy</u> and my <u>burden</u> is light. (Matthew 11:30 NIV, emphasis added)*

God will never put a burden that feels heavy on you or that would make you depressed or worried. If you are having those feelings instead of delight, then head back to Him and ask Him to take everything that is not of Him.

Let's do that right now, shall we?

Wherever you are right now, start to become more aware of His Holy Spirit inside of you and around you. Enter into His pleasure for you. Now, come to Him and ask Him to show you any burdens that He did not give you. (*Lord, show me any burdens that You did not give me.*)

You should be *seeing* a situation flash before you, or a word or phrase pop into your mind.

Now, ask the Lord to take the burden. Hand the burden to Him from your sanctified imagination.

Ask the Lord what His burden is for you to carry. Write this encounter here or in your journal so that you steward what He told you and you don't pick that old burden back up.

Steps Are Made Firm

Let's look at some other side effects that happen as we delight in the Lord.

Read the following verse slowly and take it in.

The Lord makes firm the steps of the one who delights in Him. (Psalm 37:23)

Our steps are made firm when we enjoy and delight in the Lord; we find true stability, satisfaction, and worth in Christ. It brings the focus on the eternal things of God, not temporal.

Have you ever felt like your feet were just slipping from under you or the ground was unstable, so to speak? I know I have. Those are the times a strength will come in just from delighting in Him as you put your thoughts on the unseen realm, the powered realm.

When hard times come, we dip into His pleasure of presence to hear His guidance and wisdom and get our footing back so that we are not moved.

Heart's Desires Realized

Another side effect of delighting in the Lord is the heart's desires are realized. And when your heart and God's heart are aligned, His desires and your desires become one. As you walk out these desires, His glory becomes known and shown to you and everyone around you.

Take delight in the Lord and He will give you the desires of your heart. (Psalm 37:4)

After the Womb Encounter, the delighting only increased, which means it will increase for you, too, as you step into your revelation of oneness and that inner-inner chamber time with the Lord. As I said before, you can't help but delight in Him when you are in His presence.

After the Womb Encounter, for two years, people and special speakers would all give me this same word. They all worded it slightly differently but with the same meaning. They would say something like, "God was giving you your heart's desires because you have been in His incubator dreaming with Him and delighting in Him." Over and over, I would get this word.

During that time, I would also receive words from people with Scriptures about "asking."

Ask, and keep on asking him! And you can be sure that you'll receive what you ask for, and your joy will have no limits! (John 16:24)

I would be a little baffled when I got those words because I couldn't think of one thing I had asked for or wanted to ask for, that was a desire in my heart. I felt like such a heel. (This also happens when people ask what my hobbies and interests are... I never know what to say because I don't think I have any! I just love Jesus and do what He is doing. He is my hobby.)

Finally, I said to the Lord, "Do I have desires in my heart? Because I cannot think of one." He brought to mind that I have always said I wanted to visit places like Ireland and named three other countries and cities in the U.S. It didn't sound very "holy," but I pressed into it anyway. It ended up that I was able to go to four different major places in a two-year timespan and the money came in for all of it easily.

There were more things like that that had nothing to do with typical "God-type stuff" like, taking a mission trip for Jesus, winning souls, preaching the gospel... So, for a second I had to recalibrate the way I was thinking. I was trained that all my time had to go into serving a need and the only kinds of activities that God was pleased with were the ones that were considered "spiritual." At the beginning of taking these trips, I felt sort of bad, like I had to make excuses to people when they would ask where I was going—because it was a trip serving myself, not others.

But the Lord started showing me that it *was* "spiritual" to go to these places because I was going with the Holy Spirit and was taught by Him along the way. But mostly, it was just a delightful experience that felt like a kiss from God—and He delighted in taking me there. I enjoyed and took great delight in the beauty of His creation. It was a joyous time.

When I realized that I was thinking so religiously, I shifted and felt free to say, "I'm going to this city/country because I've always wanted to go. The other reason is, because Jesus loves me and I'm His girl." I only said that second part a few times.

God wants to give you the desires of YOUR heart,

too. He doesn't just want you to be a work-bot on the earth, tirelessly preaching the gospel and having endless all-night prayer meetings. There is so much joy in the journey with Him. The places I got to go in the last few years had nothing to do with missions but had everything to do with exploring God's creation and my spiritual journey to know Him better and to find Him everywhere, not just somewhere. The more you know Him, the better you can represent Him when you *do* find yourself in opportunities to preach the gospel. I truly was given the desires of my heart. My "joy has no limits"!

Giving us the desires of our hearts is part of GOD'S DESIRES, as well. He desires to bless us and we desire to bless Him. When we spend time in the chambers of His heart, we begin to know what His dreams and desires are. Think of a human heart and how it has different chambers. I see God's chambers as many because there are many aspects to Him and He has many desires He wants to see accomplished in our world and through His Bride.

Once we know His desires and what He wants to birth around us, we then can operate from a greater level of oneness, and when ministering, always have an answer to the question that Kathryn Kuhlman would ask, "**What is the womb of Your desire, Lord?**" And in those moments, I always want to be aware of His eyes peering through mine.

When your desires are aligned with His from the chamber room, it suddenly is not about "you" anymore.

It's about "us" (the Trinity + you + the world) and what opportunities you get to step into FOR HIM to show people how awesome and powerful Jesus is. You are His Will in the flesh! You are here to make His Name famous and love people on His behalf.

The more you dive into the chambers of His heart, the more you become in sync with the ONENESS OF CHRIST and what He is doing and wants to do. You will start to understand and operate out of your truest identity: how and who heaven knows you to be.

Let's take a few minutes to delight in the Lord right now. *Thank You, Lord, for always putting me exactly in the center of Your will and constantly transforming me into an ever-maturing believer of Jesus Christ just by delighting in You.*

We never delight in the Lord to *get* something, but He always gives something in return and joy is always a byproduct. God loves to delight in you, too! It's like we take turns delighting in one another. He loves us so much. Do you feel His delight right now? Because I do. He's delighting in YOU right now.

A sidebar: You might be one who says, "God does not delight in me because He is not pleased with me." Let me ask you a question. Who told you that? God's delight in you does not depend on your actions. He sees the real you, the you He created from the womb of your momma, the *you* all of heaven believes you to be and is cheering on to walk in all the fullness of Christ Jesus. So let's take a short pit stop to demolish any lies you may be believing that are keeping you from God's delight. Ask the Holy Spirit, *"Holy Spirit, what lies have I believed in regards to Your delight in me?"* (Write it down.)

"Holy Spirit, what is Your truth regarding this?" (Write it down.)

_____
_____
_____
_____
_____
_____

"Holy Spirit, I give You the lie I was believing and I take hold of Your truth once and for all. I receive Your delight in me simply because You love me." (Picture yourself giving Jesus the lie and receiving the truth He is giving you.)

_____
_____
_____
_____
_____
_____

Now, let's get a greater revelation of the womb of His desire for the journey you are on right now. Are you ready?

REVELATORY ENCOUNTER 4

Listen to my walk-through of this encounter at:
www.GloryOnDisplay.com

Set aside at least 15-30 minutes to encounter God in a fresh way that will bring you into a deeper revelation and reality of oneness with Him. You cannot rush this.

Have your journal ready to write down everything you see and hear so that you will remember and be a good steward. (Or you can write it here on this page).

Delighting in the Lord

Let's practice delighting in the Lord first. Meditate on the verse below, and in your own words, let the Lord know your delight in Him:

Draw me into your heart.
We will run away together into the
<u>king's chamber inside of a chamber</u>.
We will remember your love,
rejoicing and <u>delighting in you</u>,
celebrating your every kiss as better than wine.

No wonder righteousness adores you!
(Song of Songs 1:4 TPT, emphasis added)

Questions to Ask Holy Spirit

What are the desires of MY heart, Lord? What are those things I have always had in my heart to do or see in this lifetime? Allow Holy Spirit to answer for you and bring up something you may have said a long time ago. (It could be from anything like "to see a city saved" to "see the Coliseum in Rome.")

_____
_____
_____
_____
_____
_____

Lord, what is the womb of Your desire in the place(s) of influence I am in right now?

_____
_____
_____
_____
_____
_____

What do I need to step out in, do, or say within this place of influence? You may have a picture of yourself doing or saying something in this place of influence.

_____
_____
_____
_____
_____
_____

Now, in your own words, take a minute to ask for these things the Lord showed you, for His desires and Your desires to come about through you so that His light can shine and His glory is displayed.

_____
_____
_____
_____
_____
_____

Until now you have not asked for anything in my name. Ask and you will receive, so that your joy will be the fullest possible joy. (John 16:24 ESV)

What to Expect Afterward

Pay attention over the next 6-12 months to the opportunities that arise that will lead you right into your heart's desires. It is His delight.

5
THE REALITY OF ONENESS

Now that you have, hopefully, had a few encounters with the Lord and He showed you a revelation of oneness, let's move to what operating in the REALITY of oneness, or moving *from* Him looks like. In other words, going from the theory of just talking about it to actually having it manifest through you here, on earth.

(If you haven't got it yet, don't worry. It's coming! The more you lean in and steward His voice, the more you will hear Him.)

Reality: *the state or quality of having existence or substance.*

In our current state of being, we have the pleasure of living in two realities or realms: the earthly realm and the heavenly realm. We are OF the heavenly realm, but we are living IN the earthly realm.

We are citizens of heaven once we become born again in Christ Jesus. But we live here, in the earthly realm until the end of this age.

As believers, we are living in a constant tension between heaven and earth until Jesus returns for His Bride. The Bible is full of tension. To name a couple of obvious ones: Jesus was, is, and is yet to come. He is all three at once! Here is another: We have all the fullness in Christ Jesus right now, but we will have the fullness when Jesus returns; it is available now but we are still learning to access and manifest it here and now.

Tension can be frustrating, especially if you are one who "feels" and "discerns" everything and everyone around you, and maybe you also have an active prophetic gifting. When heaven and earth are colliding, it can be the best and the worst of times depending on what is going on around you.

Tension is like an unresolved musical chord or note. It is like hanging in the balance, in mid-air, but crossing worlds at the same time. We must make sure to keep joy in front of us and stay grounded in the Word. Otherwise, we start to live out of our emotions and they start to control us in unholy ways. (Fear, anger, and offense, to name a few, would like to partner with you during these times. Don't do it.)

But...the exciting part about living in two worlds at once is that we can draw from the world with ALL power to manifest God's goodness into the world that has NO power. This is when His reality manifests and operates from that revelation you got of oneness. From that reality of oneness, we allow the passion of Christ for people to flow through us and with us.

If we just talk and talk and talk about our experience with the Lord and revel in it only, we will not move into the manifestation of it through our lives. But we must take action! Take risks. Step out in the new revelation and take it for a spin! Take God at His Word.

Take God at His Word

For we are His workmanship, created in Christ Jesus for good works, which God prepared beforehand, that we should walk in them. (Ephesians 2:10 NASB)

Earlier this year, the Lord was speaking to me about taking Him at His Word. He said, "How far do you want to go?" I began thinking about everything He had already written for me in heaven before I was born, all the possible things I would do in my lifetime to bring glory to His Name. We all have a choice to carry out missions He lays in front of our path. That is the way He has made us—with a freedom of choice so that we are not just robots but are freely choosing to follow Him and love Him on our own volition.

I told the Lord, "I want to carry out EVERYTHING You have written about me—all the possibilities there are, Lord."

He told me we need to **take Him at His Word** then. When there is an opportunity to pray for someone to be healed and we hear the Spirit of God whisper in our ear, "Pull that man up out of that wheelchair!" we must take Him at His Word and pull the man out of the wheelchair to be healed. How far do *you* want to go?

How far will *you* take God at His Word?

Some things get done in the prayer closet, but some get done with your own hands and feet—moving, of course, with Jesus peering through your eyes.

The more we move *from* Him, the more we are manifesting His reality into this reality.

The more we spend time *with* Him, the more REAL His reality is to us than this earthly one.

Having that set-aside time with the Lord is crucial to our lives. Did I say crucial? I mean it's a matter of life or death.

Jesus is not a reality to the world until He shows up through you.

Fill Up Before You Show Up

I am a worship leader and when I am leading worship, I always try to be aware that I am the bridge and guide between heaven and earth that day. I open doors for people to enter into heaven's realities, so it's important that I have a regular time of walking with the Lord and reading Scripture so that I am in complete alignment with Him, His will, and His desires. We do not want to just *show up* to minister to people; we want to give them God's best, not only *our* best. *Our* best is limited without God and there is no power without Him. We must keep filling up and ministering from the overflow of time spent in His presence.

The week before I lead worship to minister to God and people, I press in to prayer for the people I will be ministering to. God will show me what needs broken off or freed up so that I am able to partner with His will for His people. The Lord will also give me flashes of something I will do in the service so that I know to do it when I lead or add it to the list. Sometimes it is like a daydream that I see playing out in my mind.

Has something like this ever happened to you and you thought it was just you having a passing thought? It could be releasing a word of encouragement, saying a phrase that will set someone free, or simply going after something that's on God's heart as a congregation or at a meeting. Of course, when tapped into that realm, God does things in the moment, too, which is always exciting.

So, always fill up before you show up to minister to those around you so that the only thing leaking out of you is God's will, and you are operating from HIS reality instead of your own. And when I say "minister," I don't mean just in church. I mean at your board meetings, staff meetings, your dates, with your family, at the grocery store, or any part of your life.

Anytime we minister, we always want to bring it back to Jesus—inside and outside the church building. There will always be needs in people's lives, and often their needs are so heavy, that it would be easy to let that be the controlling factor that guides the time of ministering to them. But oftentimes, people get caught up in talking about their problems, and it becomes what they begin to worship and identify with. Eek.

What they are sharing is important, but our job is

to steer them back to Jesus and what He paid for on the cross for them to take hold of and be free from whatever ails them. (This could also apply to your secret place time with the Lord. Come remembering what He's done, not barfing up all of your woes. This will bring alignment so that you can hear the answers you may desperately need. And it may keep you from repeating bad patterns of life, as well.) This is why it is so important to fill up daily by reading the Bible and meeting with Jesus.

It's hard to take someone where you have never been. Before the days of GPS, going somewhere for the first time was a nightmare. If you got lost, you had to call someone and hope they knew the landmark you were near to guide you home! But if they had been on that road before, they could lead you home. Those were the days...ancient days.

The point is, filling up is important so that you are able to be that clear bridge between heaven and earth for the person standing in front of you and yourself. As you allow yourself to go deeper into the reality of God, you will be able to take people past their current revelation and into a revelation of their oneness with Love Himself.

When you fill up, I want you to go past that point when you think you are done. That is usually when God is able to get through the flesh. Then you will go past all the doubt, unbelief, selfish desires, masks, tantrums, and superficiality—and be thrown into a realm of His glory, His goodness, and His beauty where anything is possible. That is the place we always want to end up. Right in the lap of the Lord.

Sometimes, when I am leading worship, there can be challenges when something goes wrong in the natural realm, like the musicians playing the chorus when I am going to the bridge. Or I start a song playing the keyboard in a different key than the rest of the team. (Mary, how about a piece of humble pie while you are in the glory? Ha ha.) It can throw you right out of the realm of God in an instant!

But just as instant as this world's circumstances can knock you out of God's realm, you are one thought, one choice away from reconnecting to it. It really is that easy. I am feeling His presence right now just because we are talking about being with Him. You try it. Turn your affections on Him right now. Bask in His glory. He delights in you so much. Take a breath and bring your face to His face. How He longs for you to love on Him.

As I was trying to connect with Jesus one day, praying in tongues, I saw myself punching through my current atmosphere to try and reach Him into His atmosphere. As that was happening, the Lord started showing me how many Christians are striving to break through to get to Jesus' place and be red hot in their pursuit.

Instantly, the Lord reminded me of the Womb Encounter. With one thought and mind shift of belief, I was standing with Jesus in His womb. I am one with Him. Why was I trying to get to Him when all I had to do was remember where He and I lived?

Bringing that reality of oneness into this earthly realm requires us to yield to the Lord without controlling the situation. This can be challenging if our hunger for God turns into striving. If we want to manifest heaven on earth, we must not allow our hunger and zeal to go sideways.

Things go a little sideways when we run ahead of God and what He is doing in the moment. In our innocence, without realizing it, we become a religious control freak who wants so desperately to lead others to Christ and experience His love, but instead, end up repelling the very people we long to bring to Jesus.

We have a friend who had just learned how to heal the sick (in Jesus' name) and was so zealous about setting people free from what ails them, she could hardly contain herself! Everywhere she went, if she saw a limp, she was on that person like cinnamon sugar on an elephant ear (you know, from the State Fair?). She would hunt them down, corner them, and ask if she could pray for their injury.

There were a lot of people healed, but there were just as many who felt cornered and controlled. She then got fired from her job because she wouldn't stop taking up her co-worker's work time, hounding them to let her pray for them.

This sounds like something to celebrate if you are a *religious* person, but the fact is, she was not really the best example of the Kingdom of God being realized. She ran ahead of what God was doing. Because her hunger and zeal turned into striving without asking for

God's guidance in some of those situations, she lost her job...and probably felt like she was a martyr because of it.

Zeal is good—until you run ahead of God and you are doing things because you think you will get a gold star in heaven, or you are repelling people who really need to receive the power of God to be free. What should we ask in those opportune moments when we can bring that reality of oneness to people? "Lord, what is the womb of Your desire for this person?"

For the reality of oneness to move from theory to manifesting through us, we must be a willing vessel—and a willing vessel who obeys His voice.

Willing Vessel

Then the Spirit of the LORD clothed Gideon with power. He blew a ram's horn as a call to arms, and the men of the clan of Abiezer came to him. (Judges 6:34 NLT)

I love the story of Gideon. He was so unsure of himself that he had to get many confirmations from the Lord to believe he was chosen, but the Lord just needed a willing vessel who would give Him a "yes." God was so kind and kept reassuring Gideon to take Him at His Word, giving him confirmation after confirmation. God needed one man, Gideon, to fully trust Him in order for the Israelites to take their rightful place and stop living in oppression where everything was stolen from them.

Sounds a little bit like how *we* live—we just hide it better than they could. The enemy steals things from us all the time and leaves us dePRESSED and opPRESSED, but the Lord makes WINE out of all those PRESSES! And remember, our battle is not with flesh and blood, but with those demonic spirits that torment and try to destroy us and control us by filling our thoughts with lies.

We turn things around by renewing our minds, of course, but also being willing to step out of the lies and into the truth and trust God's way. It just takes a willing vessel like Gideon to hear, say "yes," and obey the Lord to defeat the enemy's plans.

Wouldn't you love to have experiences like arms floating down from mid-air and attaching to an armless man in the middle of a hostile country, or being translated in the middle of the night to pray for deformities in Africa like my friend, the late Dr. James Maloney has had? This is not for the faint of heart. Being a willing vessel is a blast at the end, but the beginning and middle of the story take faith in God's reality in order to carry out His blueprints.

So, I will ask you now, are you a "willing" vessel? To be a willing vessel, you must die to self, to what man's judgments are, and take the Lord at His Word. You must let the Holy Spirit "possess" you, come upon you, in a greater way as He did Gideon when the time was right. The Lord "clothed Gideon with power" and He is doing the same for you.

Once your yes is present, faith is activated and

God-manifested invades from one realm to another. Your "yes" activates faith.

Walking in His fullness would mean we are manifesting God's goodness and desires here on earth 100%. In order to operate in these revelations and gifts fully from His Spirit, we must believe that GOD'S REALITY is MORE REAL than the one we live in, and through that, we learn how to partner with Holy Spirit. But we must practice being in His reality intentionally.

I truly believe time is moving faster and faster as the Bride gets the revelation of who Jesus is and who she is in light of this knowledge. The Bride gains this knowledge through Scripture, the Holy Spirit, five-fold equippers, visions, dreams, prophecy, practicing God's presence, and more! The more she gains by the power of the Holy Spirit, the more accelerated the release of HEAVEN'S REALITY will be into every situation every minute of the day, operating in fullness.

As you begin to operate in both realities at once, mirroring who Jesus is to the world, you are DISPLAYING GOD'S GLORY.

The best way to start entering into this reality of heaven is to start with THANKFULNESS. This is where we enter the gates, right?

> *<u>Enter</u> into his gates <u>with thanksgiving</u>, and into his courts with praise: be thankful unto him, and bless his name. (Psalm 100:4 KJV, emphasis added)*

REVELATORY ENCOUNTER 5

Listen to my walk-through of this encounter at:
www.GloryOnDisplay.com

Set aside 15-25 minutes for this revelatory encounter. Every day this week, let's practice focusing on God's realm. As thankfulness increases, so does our awareness of His goodness.

As we go into this thankfulness encounter, lay any thoughts of things you have to do or take care of at His feet (you may have to picture yourself setting these things at His feet) or simply allow them to lift off of you so that you can be single-focused on Jesus.

Now, let God gaze upon your heart... Realize His delight in you, once again. As you BEHOLD HIM, His delight floods in. You are unified, moving as one.

Prayer to Partner with:

As I sit at Your feet, Lord, I cannot help but take in all Your beauty. As I drink You in, everything else seems like parched land because You are so quenching. To behold You brings ecstatic joy to my innermost being. Pull me deeper into You, knowing You, loving

You. I overflow with thankfulness for the kindness, grace, and mercy You have shown in my life. There really is no one like You, Lord.

Thank You, *for Your grace extended to me during this time I meet with You—grace to use all of my five senses to know and understand fully, what You are saying as I delight in You now. [Take a minute and thank Him for His grace.]*

Write down your encounter in your journal or in the space provided:

Lord, show me my current level of thankfulness (or gratitude) on a scale from 1-10 (1 being the lowest level).

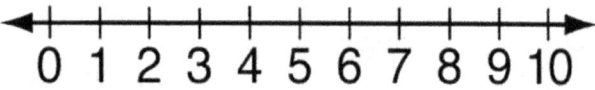

Now show me the obstacles in the road to thankfulness that need to be removed (unforgiveness, anger, selfishness, pride, etc.).

_____
_____
_____
_____
_____
_____

Lord, please remove the obstacles so that I can increase in thankfulness for all You have done and who You are.

What did He remove and how did He do it?

_____
_____
_____
_____
_____
_____

Lord, what else do You want to show me today? Is there anything I should know?

_____
_____
_____
_____
_____
_____

Let's end with thanking Him for whatever is on your heart.

_____
_____
_____
_____
_____
_____

Homework Every Day This Week

1. Wake up and say, "Thank You, Lord. I praise You." And start telling Him all the things you are thankful for (a new day with new mercies, family, friends, His love, provision, etc.).

    a. Allow that awareness to bypass your logic and reasoning and come to Him like a child.

    b. Then thank Him throughout the day as you do your job, play golf, exercise, and manage your household or your kids. (Notice, I said *or* your kids. I know it's hard to manage the house *and* the kids at the same time. I know.)

2. Pray in tongues, the language of heaven. This brings unity in the Spirit. Start out praying in the Spirit ten minutes a day and journal what shifts have taken place in you at the end of the week.

3. Fill up. Before you are around people, either to minister at church, present at a business meeting, or simply pump gas at the gas station, pray in the Spirit beforehand, and ask God to highlight a person to you and ask what He wants to tell them.

    a. As you go about your day, look for that person and deliver the message. It could be simply one word, prayer, or a sentence, but it will always be encouraging if it is from God. Maybe a Scripture will be highlighted to you, as well.

b. Ask the Lord for a picture of yourself delivering the message. (Write it down and carry it with you.)

　i. Where are you?
　ii. What color was the shirt the person was wearing?
　iii. Man or woman?
　iv. How did you deliver the message?
　v. How will the person receive it?

c. Now, take Him at His Word and BRING THE REALITY OF JESUS TO THE WORLD! This is you being God's glory on display!

What to Expect Afterwards

This is a new muscle and habit that, when formed, will be a natural thing for you to toggle between realms until you can move in both at once.

Thankfulness brings increase.

6

THE FULLNESS

Truly I tell you, whoever believes in me will do the works I have been doing, and they will do even greater things than these, because I am going to the Father. And I will do whatever you ask in my name, so that the Father may be glorified in the Son. You may ask me for anything in my name, and I will do it. (John 14:12-14)

May we press into walking in the things Jesus did and more. I will never forget when Jim and I first started pursuing the truth about the healing power of God. The driving force behind our ravenous hunger to find the truth on healing stemmed from when we were on staff at the mega-church and every Sunday during worship, we (staff/elders) had to stand up front to pray for people who needed healing, answers, miracles, etc.

But I started to notice that when people came to get prayer from us, no one ever got healed. Week after week, the same people came for prayer and NO prayers were ever answered. We had NO power. (Jim, my adorable husband, would say, "The sick get sicker when we pray for them!" Ha ha and oh my!)

But how is that the case when Jesus has ALL power and He lives in us? That's what I wanted to know!

I came to a crossroads in my faith. I told Jim, "The Bible is either true or it isn't. Are we wasting our time believing in something that isn't real?" This would've been quite the scandal if anyone else in the church knew I had these wavering beliefs, being on staff at a mega-church and all.

We searched high and low for teaching on healing, but there just wasn't much out there. Finally, someone gave us a cassette tape (yes, I said "cassette tape") by Andrew Wommack on healing. Little did we know this would change EVERYTHING. Jim started ordering every piece of material Andrew had.

I remember sitting in our sunroom, playing with the kids while listening to *You've Already Got It—So Stop Tryin' to Get It* by Andrew Wommack. It had a picture of a dog on the front cover, chasing its tail. It was a new revelation I had never heard before. It awakened something in me, something in my spirit-man; a brand new truth that my mind had not known. "What? I've already got it? You mean I can heal because I have Jesus inside of me and He is the healer? I just have to learn how to get what's inside of me out here, in this realm we live in?" Life changing.

With this new information, we could change the world! (That is probably how the disciples felt, no doubt.)

Even though this truth was already in the Bible, I had not gotten a revelation of it yet. It took another teacher (Andrew Wommack) drawing out the truest reality of it and being so spiritually open to the possibility for me to receive it.

This is what I want you to experience and see in this chapter: "You've already got it!" It is just a matter of accessing it, bringing it to manifestation in this realm, and being in such oneness with Jesus that He outshines you with every action you take.

When we read Scripture, I like to look at it as layers of revelation, sort of like an onion, only it leaves you smelling better after you eat it. Every time we read Scripture with the Holy Spirit and are open to Him teaching us, He will always show us something we didn't realize before. That is revelation. And the more you can take time to meditate on that special verse, the deeper the revelation goes into your core identity. This will also build faith muscles to believe that God's realm is more powerful, and you can access it at any time and bring it to manifestation here on earth.

We talked about starting to enter God's presence with thanksgiving, so I want us to continue going in deeper with the Holy Spirit in this concept that "we've already got it... now what?" so that we can represent the real Jesus and be GOD'S GLORY ON DISPLAY fully.

The Fullness

For in Christ all the fullness of the Deity lives in bodily form, and in Christ you have been brought to fullness. He is the head over every power and authority. (Colossians 2:9-10 ESV)

Lay aside your old Adam-self with its masquerade and disguise. For you have acquired new creation life which is continually being renewed into the likeness of the One who created you; giving you the full revelation of God. (Colossians 2:9-10 TPT)

I often find myself in intercession praying this phrase: "God, bring us into the fullness." This is that tension I was talking about earlier; how the Lord *is*, but He already *was* and is also *still coming*. The same tension is in the thought of accessing the fullness of Christ. Because we are *in Christ* we have the fullness; we have everything we will ever need.

The Bible is FULL of these types of tensions, "He was, He is, and He is to come," as I mentioned before. There are a lot of "nows" and "not yets" and "at the same times" in the Bible. God is a multi-dimensional God if you haven't figured that out yet. Past, present, and future are not as separate to Him as they are to us. He is in them all. So, while we presently have the fullness of Christ inside of us through God's Holy Spirit, we are still learning how to access it. The more we lean into making God's reality more real than this one, the more we walk in it until this kingdom looks like HIS Kingdom.

We are not walking in the complete power that is available to us...yet. Our desire and mission as believers of Christ is to move in all the things Jesus did (signs, wonders, healing, miracles, prophecy, casting out demons, carrying the fruits of the Spirit) and more. And when heaven and earth meet, there is a collision that happens between realms, as we mentioned earlier, which brings a manifestation of God's Kingdom around us. We are the faith bridge that makes that happen.

When I am leading worship, I like to imagine one of my feet in heaven and one on earth, and by the end of worship, the two realms have collided as one realm, heaven to earth as we are in Christ. Now the entire room is experiencing heaven on earth with the Creator.

You may have asked the same question I have struggled with before: "I've been pressing in and growing in this, but I do not see heaven invade or manifest in completeness (complete healings, complete miracles, complete deliverances, etc.) every single time. Why?"

That is a good and common question since this verse in Colossians says "in Christ you have been brought to fullness."

There are a few answers I could go to about this, but I think the biggest tripping hazard that keeps believers from walking in the fullness of what Jesus paid for is our earthly mindsets. The second would be that we are in the process of maturing in the knowledge and understanding of Jesus Christ.

Our mindsets have everything to do with what we believe, how much Scripture we have or have not read and meditated on, how wild our emotions are, how in control our reactions and actions are, and what lies versus truth we are believing. If our mind has not been renewed in our standard of truth, the Bible, then we have a malfunction. Have you ever had a malfunction?

When an unexpected situation comes on the scene that we were not prepared for and our mind had no holy food that day, our soul starts to react instead of our spiritual man (our spirit and Holy Spirit). That is bad news bears. That is a malfunction. The phantom "old man" that has already died (as we were reborn when we came to Christ) tries to rise back up, and we don't want to use our resurrection power to raise him back up! That phantom old nature behaves and moves opposite of the Kingdom.

Usually, when Christians are hateful and justify their bad behavior in the name of Jesus or "because God told them," it is usually the spirit of religion puppeteering them, or they have let their phantom old nature come on the scene and can't control their emotions; therefore, fear manifests into something that looks like anger, control, hate, selfishness, etc.

This is a limiting factor that keeps us from accessing the fullness of Christ. Renewing the mind leads us into truth, which activates our faith to believe anything is possible. When we believe God at His Word, the fullness of Christ starts to manifest in every situation we are in.

If you look back over church history, it seems as though it takes the church a little while to receive and then believe the teachings in the Bible—and then actually *keep* believing. All the way back to God's chosen people, Israel.

They believed in God and tore down all the idols and were *all in* for the Lord for a time. Then they would rebel and forget what God had done for them, which led to worshiping idols. Things would then go bad for them and they would cry out to God to save them and He would send someone to bring them back to their senses. They would repent again, come back to the Lord, and the cycle would start all over again.

This cycle is in many Christian lives in our day, too. Breaking this cycle calls for a renewed mind in the Word of God. Meditating on a Scripture or a chapter or a book of the Bible feeds your spirit so that it enlarges your spirit and pushes out anything that does not belong there. It also repels demons that may be knocking at the door.

The Bible says *RESIST the devil and he will flee from you*. It does not say, *chase after the devil*. Chasing the devil steals energy away from what should be used to renew the mind. To "resist" means you are standing firm like an immovable rock when something tries to move you. The rock doesn't chase things, it simply rests in the light of the sun. We rest in the light of the Son... firmly.

As you renew your mind, greater awareness of Holy Spirit inside of you awakens more and more, you mature in your understanding and knowledge of Jesus, and oneness will function at a greater and less clunky level. Faith, knowledge, and understanding grow to the point of manifesting everything Jesus paid for on the cross.

Five-Fold

I can't talk about coming into the fullness without mentioning the five-fold ministry.

> *But to each one of us grace has been given as Christ apportioned it. This is why it says:*
>
> *"When he ascended on high, he took many captives and gave gifts to his people." (What does "he ascended" mean except that he also descended to the lower, earthly regions? He who descended is the very one who ascended higher than all the heavens, in order to fill the whole universe.) So Christ himself gave the apostles, the prophets, the evangelists, the pastors and teachers, to equip his people for works of service, so that the body of Christ may be built up <u>until</u> we all reach unity in the faith and in the knowledge of the Son of God and become mature, attaining to the whole measure of the fullness of Christ. (Ephesians 4:7-13, emphasis added)*

Some are given the responsibility of being in the office of these five grace-gifts: apostle, prophet, evangelist, pastor, and teacher, to equip the body of Christ in these key areas.

BUT that doesn't mean if you are not in the office of equipping that you are out of the game by any means! And don't get jealous of those in office; the only shoes you want to walk in are the ones that were made just for you. It is not an easy ride they are on; lots of "sheep bites." Stay your course.

We are ALL called to walk in all of these giftings to a degree, and we are usually *bent* toward one or have a greater gifting in one over another, so start getting equipped in this area first.

I have found that the more you completely delight in the Lord, the more your main gifting flourishes and matures and the other giftings start to emerge, bringing you more into fullness.

As you delight in the Lord with your gift, find more ways to get equipped, grow, and exercise the other four giftings. The five-fold is here to equip and build you up, the Bible says, "**UNTIL** we reach unity in faith and knowledge in Jesus Christ and become mature, attaining THE WHOLE MEASURE of the FULLNESS of Christ—the Anointed One."

That means the five-fold is not eternally going to be equipping us. It means that the more you grow and MATURE in these five areas, the more you are like Christ, attaining the FULLNESS, THE WHOLE MEASURE of who God designed you to be.

> *Then we will no longer be infants, tossed back and forth by the waves, and blown here and there by every wind of teaching and by the cunning and craftiness of people in their deceitful scheming. Instead,*

> *speaking the truth in love, we will grow to become in every respect the mature body of him who is the head, that is, Christ. From him the whole body, joined and held together by every supporting ligament, grows and builds itself up in love, as each part does its work. (verses 15-16)*

In case you didn't know, this should be the normal MATURING Christian life. You were made to do something dangerous for the Kingdom. And you were made to mature and grow. YOU are a DISPLAY OF GOD'S GLORY.

To Advance the Kingdom, We Need to Advance

There is a beautiful progression in 1 John from CHILDREN, to YOUNG MEN, to FATHERS.

> *I am writing to you, dear children,*
>   *because your sins have been forgiven on account*
> *of his name.*
>
> *I am writing to you, fathers,*
>   *because you know him who is from the beginning.*
> *I am writing to you, young men,*
>   *because you have overcome the evil one.*
>
> *I write to you, dear children,*
>   *because you know the Father.*

I write to you, fathers,
  because you know him who is from the beginning.

I write to you, young men,
  because you are strong,
  and the word of God lives in you,
  and you have overcome the evil one.
(1 John 2:12-18)

From Children, to Young Men, to Fathers

- <u>CHILDREN</u> – If I'm at the young kid stage, I know my sins are forgiven and I know my Father.
- <u>YOUNG MAN</u> – Then the Word lives inside of me and I'm overcoming the evil one. I'm getting victories in my life. I was not overcoming before, but now I am.
- <u>FATHERS</u> – If I'm a father or mother, it says, "The fathers have known Him who has always been"—from the beginning. And I've moved to a place where God is the One who IS in every one of my circumstances now.

So, when WE ADVANCE, the KINGDOM OF GOD ADVANCES, and His glory is shown and known. We are here to make His name famous.

Our prayer should be, "Lord, advance us into maturity."

Sometimes, God pulls back the manna so that we can learn how to EAT THE MEAT. He's letting us learn how to feed ourselves because that is when we advance, when nobody is looking. When we come out of the infant or child stage in the natural, everything changes. We move from jabbering to forming words and speaking clearly. There is not a mom sticking a spoon of applesauce in your mouth once you learn how to hold a spoon. YOU FEED YOURSELF.

If He has removed the manna from your life, it is because you have advanced.

I have this picture in my mind of people who do not realize they have advanced, so they are trying to put their baby diapers back on, not realizing they already have their big boy pants on.

Oftentimes we don't even realize how much we've grown. Just peek over your shoulder right now and look back over those last six months to five years. You are not the same person.

When we do not realize we've advanced, we try to keep moving in formulas that worked in the past, and we get a little frustrated because these formulas and things are not working for us as they did before.

Then we think, "OH MY GOODNESS, I'VE LOST MY HUNGER AND CONNECTION TO GOD."

But it's actually really good news! You have advanced.

Now you just have to learn how to walk in it. As Kris Vallotton says, "(The Bible says) He is not doing the *next* thing. He is doing a *new* thing!" We need the Holy Spirit to show us how to walk in the next NEW thing.

Now it's time to be made new by every revelation that's been given to you. And you will be transformed as you embrace the glorious Christ-within as your new life and live in union with Him. (Ephesians 4:23-24 TPT)

REVELATORY ENCOUNTER 6

Listen to my walk-through of this encounter at:
www.GloryOnDisplay.com

Set aside 15-25 minutes to encounter God in a fresh way that will build your faith and identity through Scripture. The more you understand your identity, the more you walk in the fullness of the Lord.

Ask the Spirit of the Lord to be at the forefront, guiding you through these Scriptures. He is the ultimate Teacher who will bring you into all wisdom, revelation, understanding, counsel, might, and the fear of the Lord. Yes!

1. Read through all of the Scriptures below, slowly and with the intention of listening to Holy Spirit's voice.
2. Highlight or circle anything in Scripture that makes your heart beat fast when you read it or anything that speaks of Christ living on the inside of you.
3. Read through a second time and underline the benefits or positive side effects of Christ dwelling in you.

4. Take this year and meditate on the Scripture(s) that moved your heart or the ones that Holy Spirit is telling you to meditate on. Write them down on note cards and read through them before bed so that your spirit can dwell on them while you sleep.

PRAYER TO PARTNER WITH:

Holy Spirit, I ask You to lead the way. I open up my gates to receive Your revelation of the reality of oneness with You through Your Word. I lay down what I think I know. As I read these Scriptures with You, open the eyes of my heart and show me what I do not yet know.

Now, be still for a minute, pray in your spirit language (or worship Him), and meditate on the Lord before starting this revelatory encounter. As the Scripture is laid open before you, let God's voice speak to your spirit-man and mind.

And we all, with unveiled face, beholding the glory of the Lord, are being transformed into the same image from one degree of glory to another. For this comes from the Lord who is the Spirit. (2 Corinthians 3:18 ESV)

And he is the head of the body, the church. He is the beginning, the firstborn from the dead, that in everything he might be preeminent. For in him all the fullness of God was pleased to dwell, and through him to reconcile to himself all things, whether on earth or in heaven, making peace by the blood of his cross. (Colossians 1:18-20 TPT)

The mystery that has been kept hidden for ages and generations, but is now disclosed to the Lord's people. To them God has chosen to make known among the Gentiles the glorious riches of this mystery, which is Christ in you, the hope of glory. He is the one we proclaim, admonishing and teaching everyone with all wisdom, so that we may present everyone fully mature in Christ. To this end I strenuously contend with all the energy Christ so powerfully works in me. Colossians 1:26-29 (NIV)

Yes, feast on all the treasures of the heavenly realm and fill your thoughts with heavenly realities, and not with the distractions of the natural realm. Your crucifixion with Christ has severed the tie to this life, and now your true life is hidden away in God in Christ. And as Christ himself is seen for who he really is, who you really are will also be revealed, for you are now one with him in his glory! Colossians 3:2-3 (TPT)

For you have acquired new creation life which is continually being renewed into the likeness of the One who created you; giving you the full revelation of God. In this new creation life, your nationality makes no difference, or your ethnicity, education, or economic status—they matter nothing. For it is

Christ that means everything as he lives in every one of us! Colossians 3:10-11 (TPT)

Do not conform to the pattern of this world, but be transformed by the renewing of your mind. Then you will be able to test and approve what God's will is—his good, pleasing, and perfect will. Romans 12:2 (NIV)

7

TRAPDOORS

But Jesus looked at them and said, "With man this is impossible, but with God <u>all things are possible</u>." (Matthew 19:26, emphasis added)

In order to keep manifesting what is possible with God, we must visit the trapdoor conversation. I do not want to go to a negative place, but if we can see and know what trapdoors are there that keep us from displaying God's glory, we can avoid them. So, let's talk about a few of them that may keep you from walking in that full revelation of Christ in you and releasing the possibilities on God's heart in this world. And then let's de-weed them from the beautiful garden of your heart.

Relying on Human Possibility

Let's first talk about the trapdoor of relying on our human level of what is possible instead of what's possible in God's realm. I just had a conversation with someone today regarding their business. They were in the middle of a business launch and started off the launch by asking God for a certain amount of money so that a large percentage could go toward a special charity that God laid on their heart.

We need more Kingdom people like this so that more of what is on God's heart can emerge in our cities. Wouldn't you like your city to shine like the city set on a hill from Matthew 5:14-16?

> *You are the light of the world. A city set on a hill cannot be hidden. Nor do people light a lamp and put it under a basket, but on a stand, and it gives light to all in the house. In the same way, let your light shine before others, so that they may see your good works and give glory to your Father who is in heaven.*

Whatever is on God's heart is what the church and city should reflect. We need Kingdom business people who not only *allow* money to flow through them but *believe* beyond human wisdom for it so that God's Kingdom reign will expand.

Back to the story...this business owner was super pumped to believe God for this large amount—until he looked at the numbers and decided that those numbers were going to tell him the outcome. The business owner said to me, "Yeah, my Marketing Director believes we will hit the $3 million mark on new members this time around, but the numbers don't say that so far, so I am going to believe for $1 million." He got caught in the earthly realm of thinking, didn't he?

I said to him, "Wow! You are going to believe for the possible over the impossible? What is the point of believing at all if you are only going to go for the human possibilities—the lowest point?"

The business owner said, "You're right! I am going to believe for the impossible with God!"

Numbers on the screen and what we see on the earth are only one possibility. But we come from another realm. It's time to merge those two realms together for a great outcome, don't you think? Give God something to rain on and multiply.

How many times have we all been in a situation like this business person, where we chose the lowest rung on the ladder because that is what this realm, the earthly realm, tells us is possible?

This is a trapdoor: only believing what you see with your natural eyes. Be mindful of moving from God's realm when these challenges arise.

Fear of Man

We are ALL made to break what the world sees as possible and bring God's possible into it. The Bride of Christ is powerful and a representation of Jesus in this.

> *The One who breaks open the way will go up before them; they will break through the gate and go*

out. Their King will pass through before them, the LORD at their head. (Micah 2:13)

In this verse, "The Breaker" is the title for Jesus, who will rescue the Israelites.

The Breaker: the one who goes ahead, breaks down obstacles, and leads the way!

We see here our ultimate breaker is Jesus! He has broken open the way for us to be free and now we get to be His breakers for others. We are made to shatter what is possible on the earth with the greater power from the realm of the Spirit.

We are His breakers.

Part of breaking man's possibilities could look like breaking things that hold us back from our assignments. In other words, we might be called to something powerful but fear is holding us back. We need fear broken from us first to help break the fear of man in others. We then lead the way through our freedom so that others can be free and do what is impossible in man's eyes, too.

I struggled with the fear of man for many years. I was in a lot of fear and bondage of what man might think about my actions when God told me to do something or say something. I grew up under, let's just say, a little stuffy leadership that gave the impression they were always displeased with you and you needed to act mature because Jesus doesn't like laughter or strong personalities or FUN. I am not blaming them for how I ended up. At the end of the day, I am responsible for all of my choices, beliefs, and behavioral decisions. Jesus redeems everything you allow Him to. Also, they only knew what they knew at that time; it's not their fault that that is the only revelation they had of their version of Jesus: serious, boring, judgmental, proper, and angry.

But unfortunately, it created a fear of being *me* because I did not want rejection and disapproval. I let that fear clip my wings and keep me from walking in my identity for years.

When I finally broke free from it, I was at a Barbara Yoder conference called, "Release Your Sound" or something like that. When it came across my computer screen, the Lord put a prompting in me that I needed to go and said He had something to tell me. So, off I went.

During the first few sessions of worship, I stood behind a woman who was dancing and it looked like "praise aerobics" moves. (If any of you have taken Christian Aerobics back in the day, you know what I mean). I was offended and distracted. "How could this be an expression of worship to God?" I thought to myself. "This is ridiculous!"

After every session, somehow, I always ended up right behind her. My annoyance was growing. I was judging her praise and worship and deeming it soulish and not from the heart. I couldn't even worship because all I could see was HER and her offensive aerobic dancing that wasn't even "worship"! Disgusted, I kept trying to get through it all. The next session, I decided to get as far away from her as possible, so I went to the other side of the room before it all started. But to my surprise, it felt really gross over there. There was no joy, just a kind of gloomy and oppressed feeling.

In the next session, I moved back to my original side, but in a different section than I originally was so that I would not be anywhere near the dancing aerobic lady. I was safe. She was nowhere to be seen. But as soon as worship started, to no avail, this dancing maniac was all of a sudden directly in front of me…again. It didn't matter where I went, she somehow ended up right in front of me.

But something started to happen to me without even knowing it…I began drafting off of her worship dance and then swaying my body to her sway. Another song went by and then I was swaying AND moving my arms just a little. Another song went by and then I was swaying and moving my arms in full motion.

"What is happening to me?!" I thought. The more I took a step, the freer I became. The more free I became, the more fear of man was breaking and cracking off of me. The Lord said, "That lady doesn't care what man thinks of her! Only you care. But the only opinion that really matters here is Mine. She is worshiping Me with all her might. That is her truest worship."

See, we are attracted to what we are called to, even if we are critical of it at first. Or should I say, *especially* if we are critical of it at first? My spirit was attracted to this lady because of the joy and freedom she carried—because that was exactly what I was supposed to be carrying. But my soul was offended. Fear keeps us in the soulish realm and misaligned with God and His purposes.

The speaker got up to share and the message was all about breaking off, yes, you guessed it—FEAR OF MAN. One of the speakers came off the stage and started laying hands on people. He was coming right at me. "Oh no, what is he going to do?" I thought. He put his hand on my head and said something about how man had clipped my wings for years, but God was going to restore them, and then I fell out under the power of God for a while. I cried my eyes out because he had struck a chord. Something resonated in my spirit-man, breaking something loose in my soul.

The evening session was the same thing: breaking off fear of man. By the end of the night, I was broken. Fear was broken. I was FREE! When Holy Spirit came and BROKE it, I saw in the Spirit (although I didn't know I was "seeing" at that time) that I had a turtle shell on my back and Holy Spirit cracked it in half with a holy hammer! Oil was dripping from my hairline afterward. It was crazy. I will never forget it.

Now, part of my mission is to kill that spirit of fear and bring truth and life and freedom to people through being a breaker with the Holy Spirit's leading. My wings are no longer clipped or hindered. I am now that wild dancer in the river of worship, worshiping my guts out because I have been set free and leading the way of freedom for others. I hope that you will be, too! When you are the most *you*, it allows others to be the most *them*.

Sometimes, you have to draft off of other people's breakthroughs to get your own at first, but once you get your breakthrough, it's time for you to be a breaker for someone else. It's time for you to graduate to your own class to lead breakthroughs and freedom for others so that they can walk into new heavenly possibilities.

For with God, ALL THINGS ARE POSSIBLE. We were meant to bring God's possible into impossible situations.

If that were not the case, the five-fold grace gifts would not have been passed out to equip the body of Christ to do something impossible with all those tools, gifts, and weapons. So, there is no room for fear here. Fear squashes and belittles you, but courage builds and expands the true you.

Jesus walked into a town and blew people's minds when He displayed miracles and healing, but also because of how He loved the unlovely. Don't you think we were meant to love the people who are impossible to love without God?

Jesus healed sick people who came to Him because they knew He had the power to set them free from their ailments. So, don't you think we were meant to go beyond what is impossible with doctors but absolutely possible with God and set them free from sickness and disease?

If Jesus walked on the water and calmed a storm, don't you think we were meant to stand in a hurricane and bring peace to the impossible situation with our authority?

After all, Jesus told His followers they would do these types of things, plus greater.

I could go on and on with all the things Jesus did. I trust you to read them for yourselves. Find all the things Jesus did in the Bible that you have not seen yet with your own hands and start asking the Lord for those opportunities.

It is a release of God's goodness. And don't forget, we do this *with* the Lord, through His eyes from the place of oneness to be a wonderful display of His glory.

So, do not fall into this trapdoor of the fear of man.

Disappointment

Some people do not want to believe for God to do the impossible because they are afraid of being disappointed. This is another trapdoor: disappointment.

The invisible shield of self-protection is raised up and it looks like we are believing, but our actions speak otherwise. I think sometimes we are *hoping* for something impossible to happen with God, but we are not really putting any faith behind it and believe that it will actually happen. Faith is the substance of things *hoped* for, the evidence of things not seen (see Hebrews 11:1).

Disappointment can actually muck up your spiritual telephone line to and from the Lord. It is like opening a door to your spiritual connection and saying, "Come on in, demons! You are invited to speak into my life and tell me lies that make me feel like what I am doing is right."

I partnered with disappointment a few years back because God did not move how I wanted Him to or thought He would move. We had a week-long nightly gathering of worship and prayer called "Catch the Wave." Some staff members felt we needed to press in for a week and open the doors for God to move every night. I was as hungry as I could be (striving), expecting manifestations, maybe Jesus to appear in the flesh... I was expecting something amazing to happen.

But by the fourth night, nothing was happening—and, I'm pretty sure the Dove flew away! By the last night, I had given up and was heartbroken and very disappointed. I didn't realize it at the time, but I was offended by God. Have you ever experienced something similar?

Well, this shut me down...so far down... I didn't even realize it for months. I was not connecting with God like I used to or stepping out anymore. I was so frustrated and it felt like I had lost something.

After the disappointing week of God not showing up how I thought He would, I had raised up that invisible self-protection shield against God and against stepping out and taking risks for God so that I didn't get disappointed again. I let God into *some* parts of my heart, but I was offended by Him and started questioning some things. Let's just say I was not in a good place.

That spirit of disappointment takes over when you let it and it's like you are not even the same person anymore. It is like you are watching yourself behave terribly and you can't stop it. It was like the real me was caged on the inside and couldn't seem to break back out.

So, one of my friends gave me a tough love conversation that slapped me in the face spiritually. It was like blinders slid off my mind and I realized I had partnered with disappointment and was offended by God and how it was linked to that Catch the Wave week.

So, with tears and a hurt heart, I finally decided to ask the Lord the big question I had been avoiding: "God, why didn't You show up that week? We poured everything out. I poured everything out to You—everything I had."

His answer was sovereign.

"Mary, I AM GOD," He said. "I can move however I want, whenever I want."

At that moment, a revelation hit me that I was treating the Lord like my own personal dog to have Him do tricks. His answer did not offend me; His answer stopped me in my tracks, and I felt the fear of the Lord, probably for the first time in my life.

He is I AM.

I was grieved to think I was treating Him like my dog that I could order around. Even though for the next few months, the Lord was helping me dig myself out of my grave, my connection to the Lord in the spiritual realm was muddy and hard to hear. I felt drawn to attend a Patricia King conference.

During the conference, I asked the Lord why I still felt blocked from my connection with Him. He showed me my line to heaven in the spirit realm. It was like a telephone line going vertically from me to heaven. On it were a bunch of little critters (demons) that had junked it up and stuck to it, muddying my connection with God. They were just hanging on my line having a good time.

This is what happens when we open the doors to disappointment, fear, doubt, offense, unforgiveness, sin, etc. We blame the devil a lot for the things that we have actually allowed or given permission to come in because of the agreements we have made when we partner with disappointment (or whatever else isn't from God).

Sometimes you've got to "clean house" because bad decisions or partnerships will attract those critters and they need to be kicked out.

So, I grabbed hold of the line (physically, like it was in the natural realm) and with my hand, I swiped upwards and told those critters to "be gone, in the Name of Jesus!" and they all flung off. It's that easy.

> *Simon Peter said to him, "Lord, not my feet only but also my hands and my head!" Jesus said to him, "The one who has bathed does not need to wash, except for his feet..." (John 13:9-10)*

Sometimes walking through life, you pick up dirt and you don't need to be saved again, just a regular cleaning.

Don't let one thing hold you back from who God made you to be by falling into this trapdoor of disappointment! I mean, what are we living for if we are not believing God for something impossible that will expand His Kingdom's reign?

Don't get caught in the trap of holding on to your self-righteous disappointment, unforgiveness, offense, or whatever it is you might be holding. It is a net from the enemy, and he is using you to do his bidding when caught.

If we want to go ALL IN with the Lord, we have to knock down the wall of self-protection and turn from anything else keeping us from being the TRUE BREAKERS OF MAN'S POSSIBILITIES and bring them into believing supernaturally with God. His way is always better.

I want to see cities saved. And it starts with us first, having the inward glory by breaking partnerships with things we have let attach to us that are not of God (fear, disappointment, anger, sin, etc.).

Then there is an outward display of His glory where you come fully alive, fully courageous, fully present, and fully YOU to break earthly possibilities.

In the words of Mary Jane from Spiderman, "Go get 'em, Tiger!"

REVELATORY ENCOUNTER 7

Listen to my walk-through of this encounter at:
www.GloryOnDisplay.com

Set aside 15-25 minutes to walk through this prophetic act of clearing your spiritual telephone line to heaven and letting God take away anything that is not from Him.

Remember to journal your encounter or write about it on the page below.

First, let's break off partnership with anything that is not of God. You can pray your own prayer or join mine below.

Dear Lord, I break off partnership with anything I have partnered with that is not of You. Today, it ends. I fully trust in You and all of Your ways. I know You have plans and purposes for my life and I want to walk fully in all of them. I put down every invisible self-protection wall so that I can connect with You fully in this moment.

Keep your mind with the Holy Spirit and ask,

Holy Spirit, what have I been partnering with that has been sabotaging my life? Are there critters hanging on my spiritual line? Sit quietly until you hear Him speak or He gives you a picture in your mind's eye.

Prayer to Partner with:

Please forgive me for partnering with something other than You. I repent. I turn from that partnership and partner with Holy Spirit only.

NOW, STAND UP. Grab your (spirit) line to heaven as a prophetic act and on the count of three, let's swipe it in an upward motion while saying, "**BE GONE, in the Name of Jesus!**" One, two, three... **BE GONE, in the name of Jesus!**

Praise Him.

- *Holy Spirit, what might be one or two things I am called to be the "breaker" in, in order to free others?*
  - *Is there anything that needs to break in me right now in order to carry this out?* (If so, ask the Lord to break it right now.)

_____
_____
_____
_____
_____
_____

Holy Spirit, what impossibilities are You calling me to bring into manifestation on the earth?

_____
_____

Lastly, let's see how your garden is growing!

Holy Spirit, if I am a garden, what do You see blooming?

Lord, would You please expound on that?

8

SET APART

Holiness. When I used to hear that word, I would think of strict rules, long hair, no make-up, long skirts, and no fun. Isn't it just like the devil to twist people up to display something so opposite of God?

Being holy is not about following a bunch of rules (that ended when Jesus died and rose and fulfilled the law), or dressing in a certain style, or even growing your hair long like a Nazarite, but rather a natural reaction to the action of being a lover of God. Being holy is being set apart for the Lord and His will. As we are in God's presence, it provokes us to live set apart because our love for Him is so strong; we would never want to hurt His heart or take advantage of His grace. It's just not natural to sin when your life is embedded in Love Himself; you never want to hurt His heart. It IS natural to live a life of being holy as He is holy when you are living out of your oneness with Christ completely.

Have you ever felt like you just didn't fit in? I always thought something was wrong with me because I was never in the *cool crowd* in my teen years. Not only that, I was drawn to the down and outers or that one lonely person. Those kids who were on drugs and dressed a little gothic and raggedy, walking around depressed, skipping class... I was also a band nerd, so there is that.

There was something in me that felt compassion toward these loners and a hand reaching out to pull them from their lonely pit. These were my friends. A lot of them were hurting from bad home life situations and didn't have parents like I had to guide them out of it.

I put myself in these situations that my parents would never have approved of, yet it was like I was shrouded and safe from evil. I watched all these things happen around me and was never afraid—but knew I did not belong there. I did not belong in the middle of sin because I no longer had a sinful nature; I was set apart. I did not need those types of friends in my life, but they needed me. I was able to minister as much as I was let in. I am not sure what happened to all of them, but I pray many seeds were planted in their hearts toward the Lord.

There was a point, a crossroad, when I went away to college where the road kept getting narrower and narrower. I could no longer straddle the fence, so to speak, and put myself in compromising situations that were clearly sinful. The Lord was refining me the older I got. There is a grace when we are young in the Lord, to learn and grow and make choices; but we were made to learn from those situations in order to keep advancing and maturing into who God made us to be.

Once your life was full of sin's darkness, but now you have the very light of our Lord shining through you because of your <u>union</u> with him. Your mission is to live as children flooded with his revelation-light! And the supernatural fruits of his light will be seen in you—goodness, righteousness, and truth. Then you will learn to choose what is beautiful to our Lord. (Ephesians 5:8-10 TPT, emphasis added)

The more I allowed myself to be set apart, the more I grew in the Lord. But I still needed to grow in love. That came later, unfortunately. There was a trail of dead bodies in my past because I was SO set apart and unwilling to bend. I killed their souls and our relationships! I felt if I changed HOW I was, that it would change WHO I was. I couldn't be further from the truth on that thought! Years later, I finally realized that everyone communicates and receives communication in their own unique way. I always thought I was compromising if I spoke to people any other way but directly because that is how I am wired. I liked people to say what they were trying to say and not beat around the bush, so I thought that is what they wanted from me too. Once I realized this was not the case, I started to operate from a place of love and communicate in a way people could receive what I was saying and what God wanted to say through me.

First Corinthians 13:1 (NIV) says, "If I speak in the tongues of men or of angels, but do not have love, I am only a resounding gong or a clanging cymbal..."

A mission from the Lord without love is lost. There

is no representing the Lord without love. I know people who are so uncompromising to the Lord's missions but are so unloving and so exclusive, that their favor with man is limited. We need both favor with God and favor with man to accomplish His will on the earth.

When we are willing to bend and let love lead the missions, we begin stepping into our truest identity, which is how heaven sees us and has made us to be from the first conceptual thought God had of us.

So, being set apart for the Lord should never be so uncompromising that love is not at the forefront. Jesus is Love. Being set apart also does not mean you are alone, although it can be a lonely place. When you are a forerunner for the expansion of God's Kingdom here on earth, it sometimes feels like no one understands you or what you are doing. You even look a little *loco* to some.

But remember this: When a new thought or new invention comes into the world, there is always some resistance because people have not seen what you have seen. They have not had the visions you have had, the understanding, the revelation, the knowledge, the message. See, everything is amplified in the Kingdom of God for those who believe: wisdom, knowledge, inventions, ideas, solutions, etc., so do not be surprised when people don't understand your mission completely. Ask the Lord for the right way to present the vision so that people can see it with you and help you accomplish it.

God's Glory on Display

Fruit of the Spirit

I have been asking the Lord what the Bride was supposed to be doing and what does a holy, set-apart, Bride of Christ look like?

I followed the breadcrumbs that led me back to verse 22 of Galatians 5 (NLT):

The Holy Spirit produces this kind of fruit in our lives: love, joy, peace, patience, kindness, goodness, faithfulness, gentleness, and self-control.

If we are walking in God's Holy Spirit, we should be producing this fruit because it is a byproduct of His nature. If we are eating of Him regularly, we should be a display of love, joy, peace, patience, kindness, goodness, faithfulness, gentleness, and self-control.

But I didn't feel like I was displaying these things very well, so I was thinking about studying each fruit a month: love, joy, peace, patience, kindness, goodness, faithfulness, gentleness, and self-control. But something kept stopping me from "organizing my studies" on it.

One morning, I was talking to the Lord about this. He led me to John 15:4-5 (ESV):

Abide in me, and I in you. As the branch cannot bear fruit by itself, unless it abides in the vine, neither can you, unless you abide in me. I am the vine; you are the branches. <u>Whoever abides in me and I in him, he it is that bears much fruit</u>, for apart from me you can do nothing. (emphasis added)

It hit me that I was trying to produce fruit another way (by researching each word) when all I had to do was go back to abiding in Him and Him in me. It is a supernatural flow and law of production where fruits of the Spirit are manifested as we abide in Christ. When we abide, fruit is inevitable. When we do not abide, fruit is impossible.

When we are producing the fruit of the Spirit, it is a good sign we are living a life set apart. And this comes out of the place of oneness in Him. The more we are with Him, abiding in Him, the more we operate *as* Him, reflecting His reality in our daily lives on earth. All roads lead back to spending time in His presence and living out of our oneness with Christ.

Deeper Levels of Oneness

When I go into the inner-inner chambers of the Lord, that place of the womb of Christ, I am always overwhelmed as He shows me how much more there is to come into, to explore in Him and about Him.

One day, as I was with the Lord thinking about oneness in the Spirit, I saw He and I together and He grabbed my hand and swooped me around in a dance. It was like we were moving and spinning and twirling as ONE spirit in unity. We both looked translucent, so I knew He was making a point about us moving as one Spirit. I knew that if I kept going deeper in this revelation of oneness, we could move as one Spirit all the time. So, I asked the Lord, "How do I access a deeper level of oneness with You?"

Here is what He said:

Set apart your eyes, ears, hands, and feet. What you take in and give out; be selfless. Selfish desires are always knocking at your door. But if you truly want to access the moving together in one Spirit, selflessness is the key along with making your body and time a conduit for My Spirit to talk through, walk through, see through, and be through.

At first, when He said the words "set apart," it kind of triggered me because I remembered the days of the fiery preachers yelling at me to be more on fire for Jesus and set myself apart. Do more, hunger more, try more!

So, I challenge you, if you are in the same boat as I was with that phrase, "set apart," that you join me in laying down the old memories and creating new ones with the Lord now. We cannot judge everything based on how someone in our past acted or reacted in trying to bring people to Jesus. We only know what we know until we know something different. This is why it is so important to stay in the secret place with the Lord: so we receive the unfolding revelation and truth of who He really is. (Of course, with the Bible as our anchor!)

Back to what the Lord is saying to us: *Set apart your eyes, ears, hands, and feet.* He wants us to be mindful of what we allow to come through our senses and out of our mouths and actions.

I had been watching this TV show about people

with powers who could control fire, earth, water, and air. But when the first season was over, the late Dr. James Maloney came to me in a dream and he said, "Stop watching that show. You are opening yourself up to the wrong kinds of possibilities!"

Whoa. Sometimes we need prophets to come to us in our dreams to say it plainly when we just aren't getting it, apparently. We are not of this world. We are citizens of heaven, born of the Spirit, and we carry power straight from God, the Father, the most powerful entity inside and outside of time itself. We have His seed and His seal.

Because of this, we are drawn to TV shows like this or mystical powers sometimes because we are created to do the things we have not yet seen on earth. But this is man's version and the devil's version of what is possible, not God's. If we want to see real power in our lives, all we have to do is follow Jesus; say what He says to who He wants to say it to; heal broken bodies that stand before us and want to be healed; set demonically oppressed people free; be a servant; help the poor, orphans, widows; and love the unlovely, to name a few.

Our problem is, we keep looking for something more exciting than the life we live, not realizing how exciting God is and the assignments He gives us. If you want excitement, TAKE A RISK with Holy Spirit's voice every day.

Afraid it's not going to work when you take a risk and you will look like a fool? Then look like a fool and keep going back to the secret place and enjoying the

Lord until it works. Sometimes our flesh needs to break down so that our spirit-man can lead it. Humility protects us from getting arrogant or thinking this is in any way our strength. The Lord makes Himself most known when we are most dependent on Him.

Set apart your eyes, ears, hands, and feet, and see how much power you walk in.

Set apart your life as holy unto Him. That just means to make choices that display His Kingdom and His character and His love. We complicate God so much sometimes when it is so simple to come into Him and know him.

He then said, *selfLESSness is the key along with making your body and time a conduit for My Spirit to talk through, walk through, see through, and be through.*

I asked the Lord how to be more selfLESS. Here is what He said:

1. Stop letting time rule you. You rule your time.
2. Spend more time with Me in the stillness.
3. Find at least one person to serve every week (especially the widows, orphaned, and poor).
4. Become/own who I have created you to be; fully blooming in your gifts, callings, and authority. No holding back or apprehension.

It is always good to ask the Lord how to do something so that we don't waste time doing unfruitful things. His answers are always way better than ours!

REVELATORY ENCOUNTER 8

Listen to my walk-through of this encounter at:
www.GloryOnDisplay.com

Set aside 15-25 minutes to encounter God in a fresh way that will bring you into a deeper revelation and reality of oneness with Him.

Have your journal ready to write down everything you see and hear so that you will remember and be a good steward (or you can write it here on this page).

Ask Holy Spirit:

Holy Spirit, do I feel a lack in any of these areas: love, joy, peace, patience, kindness, goodness, faithfulness, gentleness, or self-control?

[Take a minute and allow Him to show you a moment in your life where He displayed the fruit that you feel you are lacking in. As we recognize what He puts on display in those moments, we then reflect His actions because we are one with Him, lacking in nothing.]

Holy Spirit, how do I access a deeper level of oneness with You?

In order for me to be set apart for You, what are You calling me to do, change, get rid of, or rearrange...

...in my eyes?
...with my ears?
...with my hands?
...and with my feet?

Take a few minutes and ask about each one.

What resources are You leading me to that will help me grow in that deeper level of oneness with you (places, books, podcasts, etc.)?

_____

_____

_____

_____

_____

Homework

Being selfless leads to thinking of others above ourselves. It is the way Christ Himself thought, even though He was the King over everyone. He was known as the greatest servant of all when He gave His life for another: you and me.

When was the last time you did a selfless act and put someone else's needs above your own?

Ask Holy Spirit:

Is there a specific person You want me to reach out to this week and meet a need? Who?

If He does not give you a name, ask the Holy Spirit to bring you opportunities to serve someone, meeting *their* needs above your own this week.

What to Expect Afterward

You should feel no more lack as you move in your oneness with Jesus and reflect His actions.

This week, keep your eyes peeled for the special person God highlighted to you.

When you serve, do it as unto the Lord, like you are serving God Himself—because you are. Don't worry about them thanking you. But if they do, offer it up to the Lord as incense the next time you meet with Him. It is praise to Him.

9

KISS & TELL

I had a dream where I was a witness to corruption in the fire department. The higher-ups and others in the department killed a man who had a wife and a son. I watched the entire thing play out from where the bad guy had the bomb, to bringing it in the building where the victim was. I yelled at the victim to run as I ran out the door, but I turned around after I got out of the building and he was just standing at the glass door, staring at me like he couldn't get out. I don't know why he didn't push the lever to get out. Maybe it was locked? The bomb went off and blew him up with the rest of the building and the bomber.

As I walked briskly down the sidewalk with the widow immediately after it happened, shaken up and outraged by the corruption and murder of her husband, we came to a restaurant where the higher-ups were all sitting in uniform at a table. I told them I knew what they had done, and I pointed to one person at the table and told them I saw them there helping to plant the bomb and murder the victim. They seemed scared and surprised. I would walk past a few more people, and I would tell the ones who I saw plan this that I was a witness, and I would tell everyone what they had done.

I was not scared, but bold. I told them all I had **seen** and I had **heard** conversations of them plotting. They were scared because they knew they were all caught.

When I woke up, I thought to myself, "Wow, we can be a witness for something good or something bad." I was thinking about the disciples in the Bible. After they saw Jesus do miracles, preach freedom from the law, and cast out demons, they were the witnesses who **saw** and **heard** everything.

We are the witnesses of Jesus. We are here to tell everyone what *already* happened and what *is* happening and what is *going* to happen. When I witness a miracle, say, a hip being completely healed and the person throwing out their walker, I display it as a trophy and tell anyone who will listen what Jesus did. I am His witness and so are you.

I know there are other aspects of this dream God is probably showing you, but I only want to talk about what He showed me as far as seeing and hearing.

Seeing and hearing are very important among believers of Christ because God still speaks and still does miracles today. Despite what you grew up being taught, nothing has "passed away." That is garbage theology to take the parts out that you don't understand or haven't seen and keep only some parts of the Bible and make them fit into your life only if they don't scare or embarrass you. Garbage.

We can see and *hear* in the spirit realm because when we became born again, Holy Spirit, God's VERY Spirit, was deposited inside of our being.

> *"For in him we live and move and have our being." As some of your own poets have said, "We are his offspring." (Acts 17:28 NIV)*

> *Don't you know that you yourselves are God's temple and that God's Spirit dwells in your midst? (1 Corinthians 3:16)*

His Spirit is here to teach us, and communicate to us, what Jesus would say or do.

> *...He (Holy Spirit) will guide you into all the truth. He will not speak on his own; he will speak only what he hears, and he will tell you what is yet to come. He will glorify me because it is from me that he will receive what he will make known to you. All that belongs to the Father is mine. That is why I said the Spirit will receive from me what he will make known to you. (John 16:13-15)*

> *Then the disciples came to Him and said, "Why do You speak to them in parables?" And He replied to them, "<u>To you it has been given to know the secrets and mysteries of the kingdom of heaven,</u> but to them it has not been given." (Matthew 13:10-11 AMP, emphasis added)*

Jesus spoke in parables to reveal God's secrets and vision, and because we, His followers who have been born again, have His Spirit inside of us, we are equipped with the eyes to see, ears to hear, and hearts to understand what He is saying. Jesus was constantly unveiling the wisdom and mysteries of God, and to this day, God's wisdom and mysteries are still being unveiled by Holy Spirit for us to see, hear, and take hold of. We just have to pay attention and seek Him to find it. He wants to be found, and He wants His mysteries and vision to be found.

As we press in to see in the Spirit, hear in the Spirit, and understand the heart of the Father, we cannot help but manifest His goodness and love around us. We find ourselves laying hands on the sick and seeing them recover. We find ourselves speaking God's kind of wisdom out of our mouths we did not know we knew. We find ourselves serving the poor, the needy, the widows, and the single parents because a heart that seeks God is provoked to serve others and love others as Jesus would.

The more you grow, the more you witness what Jesus will do through a normal person like you. The more you witness these things, the more you believe. The more you believe, the more you tell. When God's hand moves through you, it's like a kiss from heaven. "Kiss and Tell" is not a bad thing in this case. The world needs you to be His witness of what He has done, what He is doing, and what He wants to do for them.

I want to be His witness, don't you? I want to **see** His

hand at work and I want to **hear** what He is saying so that I can multiply His Kingdom on the earth!

Known Among Christians or Known Among Sinners?

In order to bring Jesus out of the closet and display His Light as a witness, we want to be in the right place at the right time as much as possible.

We had been house shopping for months because we had some things coming and changing that required us to need the extra space. Over our 27 years of marriage, we have moved about 12 times, (due to real estate investments, relocation, job change, Jesus, etc. I knew you were wondering.). We consider ourselves agents of the Lord and will go or stay wherever He says and have done that all of our married life and will continue to do that. But...our hope is this would be the last move. I believe I cried during our last move because it was so stressful.

As I was saying, we had been looking at what to do next to fit our needs for this season of life: build or buy. We had the option of two houses before us.

House #1: This property was in a great neighborhood with larger yards and you would not have to talk to your neighbor if you did not want to. It feels like a retreat neighborhood. We would need to build a house on these lots and would get exactly the house we want and "need."

House #2: This option before us is a model home

(already built) in a neighborhood with a tiny yard, so close to the neighbors you could touch their house out of your window, no privacy, but all the upgrades you can imagine inside the house and the front porch of my dreams. The model home house is in a neighborhood that is very active and made for convenience. It is called "City Life in the Suburbs." There will be shops, food, and ice cream parlors you can walk to because it is for the neighborhood. (They had me at "ice cream" and "walk.") And you would pretty much be *forced* to talk and meet your neighbors (who do not know Jesus) because of this active lifestyle and close proximity to one another.

Jim and I discussed this at length one morning, listing all the pros and cons. The hide-away property or the no-privacy property? I walked away from our conversation not knowing which to choose. I felt confused and a little tortured. I told the Lord, "You know exactly what we need and where we are supposed to be. Help us, Lord."

I then heard this question: "Do you want to be known among Christians or do you want to be known among sinners?"

I began to have flashes of all the places we travel and Jim speaks and how often people want to move here to be a part of what God is doing among us. It makes us feel good, like we are doing a good job at equipping and training the saints, which is our desire. You may not admit it, but when people want to be around you, it feeds your soul. But is it our *soul* we are in need of feeding? Maybe sometimes, but usually if your spirit-man is filled up, it feeds and leads your soul.

I know you are dying to know where the story ends...so here we go.

We chose neither. For about a week, we decided peace was on neither house. So we decided to look one more time at listings. Through a series of events, prayer, and prophetic words, we uncovered a house that had been on the market for six months (which is unheard of right now) that had been hidden from us before. On a whim, we toured the house on a day like any other, not expecting to buy it. To our surprise, it was in the same neighborhood as House #2. We just shook our heads. We could not get away from this neighborhood. As soon as we walked in, Jim said, "This is it!" I agreed and we closed soon after.

The house is exactly what we needed for this time in our life and the neighborhood is our assignment. People here need us and they need the Holy Spirit in us. Our prayer is that unbelievers around us feel loved and see God's glory on display, thus drawing them to Jesus.

God is always searching for those who will wait on Him, those who will love, care for, and sacrifice time, money, resources, and even houses to save many people from hell and to bring them into His Kingdom family...to be His witness.

If you have been in a place of indecision, ask the Lord to show you anything (ways of thinking) you need to lay down first in order to move to the next assignment He has for you.

I don't know about you, but I want to be known among sinners more than I want to be known among Christians—but more importantly, I want to make Jesus famous and known among sinners. It sounds like a Christian answer, but I truly mean it. Let's unlock the works of God's hand inside of you.

REVELATORY ENCOUNTER 9

Listen to my walk-through of this encounter at:
www.GloryOnDisplay.com

Set aside 15-25 minutes for this revelatory encounter. Have your journal ready to write down everything you see and hear so that you will remember and be a good steward (or you can write it here in this book).

Unbelievers need to *see* AND *hear* about the works of God's hand. These works are churning inside of you, waiting to be released to set captives free, let the brokenhearted be healed, and lost souls be brought to the Kingdom of God. Let's unlock the works of God's hand inside of you.

Prayer to Partner with:

Holy Spirit, I thank You for living inside of me and always reminding me of my righteousness before the Lord. I lay before You any limiting beliefs I have had in the past. My strength and power come from You and You alone. Holy Spirit, I ask You to churn up the gifts inside of me, the power of God inside of me, the power of God's love inside of me, Your compassion to see people set free at the sound of a word or a touch from You. God, I want to see the captives set free! I want Your name to be made famous through me and my willingness to be Your witness. I turn from limiting beliefs, and I ask for an exchange of those limiting beliefs for Your Spirit of revelation, insight, and understanding. I ask for a discerning spirit in every situation to come. May my life shine and attract the ones groping in the darkness, looking for light. Show me where to cast my net and gather the pre-disciples, Lord. I ask this in the mighty name of the One who saved me, Jesus Christ.

Questions for Holy Spirit

Lord, do I have any wrong beliefs about what it means to be Your witness? If so, what are they?

_____
_____
_____
_____
_____
_____

Give any wrong beliefs to the Lord, LIKE YOU ARE HANDING THEM TO HIM.

Ask Him what beliefs He would like to give you instead.

Receive what He is giving you.

_____
_____
_____
_____
_____

Would You please give me a vision of the assignment before me that I am walking into and the season/assignment I will advance to next?

_____
_____
_____
_____
_____

Who do I need to become during this season?

_____
_____
_____
_____
_____

Lord, where are the pre-disciples in my world/sphere of influence? Where should I cast my net this week, next month, this year?

_____
_____
_____
_____
_____
_____

What works of Your hand have I witnessed?

_____
_____
_____
_____
_____
_____

Bring someone to mind that I should share the things I have witnessed and the good news of YOU. (Make sure you follow through on this one.)

_____
_____
_____
_____
_____
_____

Write down any further encounters or words God spoke to you.

10

PRIESTLY KINGS AND KINGLY PRIESTS

There are two anointings people are *bent* toward: priestly and kingly. To walk in complete oneness, we must not be one or the other, but rather, both. Let's break down the two and see what pings you.

Some of you are built like a priest.

The priestly anointing is the intimacy, intercession, angelic, prophecy, healing, evangelism, raising the dead, changing the atmosphere, soaking, time in His presence, etc. The priests open the gate between heaven and earth for the kings to do their part.

Some of you are built more like a king.

The kingly anointing is to defend, protect, conquer, build, administer, and advance to take territory so that what the devil has possession of is taken back and heaven invades earth in that part of their sphere of influence, etc. Kings have resources. They have plans and strategies. They have goals. Kings have affluence and influence within a sphere of authority.

This is not an exhaustive list by any means, so no one get offended if I didn't list something you felt passionate about.

Jesus' intention was to create a people who would establish His Kingdom with authority on earth, but do it from a priestly heart.

> *But you are God's chosen treasure—priests who are kings, a spiritual "nation" set apart as God's devoted ones. (1 Peter 2:9 TPT)*

In the new covenant, you get to be both. You are priestly kings or kingly priests. You have permission to be both, kingly AND priestly. After all, Jesus is both King of all kings and our great High Priest, so shouldn't we be, too?

King David is the best example in the Bible of someone who operates in both, kingly and priestly.

> *Then the LORD said, "Rise and anoint him; he is the one." So Samuel took the horn of oil and anointed him in the presence of his brothers, and from that day on the Spirit of the LORD came upon David in power. (1 Samuel 16:13)*

David was an anointed musician who, when he played the harp, would drive the evil spirit away and cease the harassment King Saul was enduring. That would be the priestly side of David. The psalms are filled with David interceding, praising, singing, and ministering to God in song and dance.

The first time we see the kingly side of David is in 1 Samuel 17. Goliath had been taunting and making fun of the Israelite army and making fun of God. David came from tending the field of sheep to bring a snack for his brothers when Goliath was taunting the armies of God. David heard this and decided to be the one to step up, defend God's name, and kill Goliath.

David said to Saul, "Let no one lose heart on account of this Philistine; your servant will go and fight him." Saul replied, "You are not able to go out against this Philistine and fight him; you are only a young man, and he has been a warrior from his youth." But David said to Saul, "Your servant has been keeping his father's sheep. When a lion or a bear came and carried off a sheep from the flock, I went after it, struck it and rescued the sheep from its mouth. When it turned on me, I seized it by its hair, struck it and killed it. Your servant has killed both the lion and the bear; this uncircumcised Philistine will be like one of them, because he has defied the armies of the living God. The Lord who rescued me from the paw of the lion and the paw of the bear will rescue me from the hand of this Philistine." (1 Samuel 17:32-37)

Meanwhile, the Philistine, with his shield bearer in front of him, kept coming closer to David. He looked David over and saw that he was little more than a boy, glowing with health and handsome, and he despised him. He said to David, "Am I a dog, that you come at me with sticks?" And the Philistine cursed

David by his gods. "Come here," he said, "and I'll give your flesh to the birds and the wild animals!"

David said to the Philistine, "You come against me with sword and spear and javelin, but I come against you in the name of the Lord Almighty, the God of the armies of Israel, whom you have defied. This day the Lord will deliver you into my hands, and I'll strike you down and cut off your head. This very day I will give the carcasses of the Philistine army to the birds and the wild animals, and the whole world will know that there is a God in Israel. All those gathered here will know that it is not by sword or spear that the Lord saves; for the battle is the Lord's, and he will give all of you into our hands."

As the Philistine moved closer to attack him, David ran quickly toward the battle line to meet him. Reaching into his bag and taking out a stone, he slung it and struck the Philistine on the forehead. The stone sank into his forehead, and he fell face down on the ground. So David triumphed over the Philistine with a sling and a stone; without a sword in his hand he struck down the Philistine and killed him. David ran and stood over him. He took hold of the Philistine's sword and drew it from the sheath. After he killed him, he cut off his head with the sword. When the Philistines saw that their hero was dead, they turned and ran. (1 Samuel 17:41-51)

If that is not kingly, I don't know what is! Defeating armies and claiming land is some pretty kingly stuff.

David could walk in the priestly and the kingly at any given moment. This carried through to the rest of his life, even when it looked like he would never step into the official title of king. He still trained himself in the ways of the Lord and the skills of battle and trained mighty men in the same way. Eventually, David sat in the seat of king, but also reigned in the manner of a priestly man after God's own heart.

> *And David danced before the Lord with all his might, wearing a priestly garment. So David and all the people of Israel brought up the Ark of the Lord with shouts of joy and the blowing of rams' horns. (2 Samuel 16:14-15)*

I am also reminded of Moses, who led all of Israel through possibly the roughest time of their entire lives for 40 years in the wilderness. I love how Moses went to the top of the mountain to speak with God, get His mandates and direction, and then lead the people. This is a kingly and a priestly display, as well. In the same way, we are called to go up into the presence of God and come back from that presence with strength and strategy. This is a display of God's glory.

Drawing from Both

It took a very long time for Jim and me to figure out the revelation and benefit of being a king and a priest in our marriage.

He is bent more toward king, and I am bent more

toward priest. Here is what it would look like in our marriage at times. Maybe you can relate.

Sometimes, we would judge one another when we weren't approaching situations, or even the church for that matter, the same way. I thought he should spend 12 hours on his face before making a decision and he thought I needed to get up off the floor and make the decision.

On vacation, he had a book called *All About Asset Allocation* and mine was called *Moving in Glory Realms*.

There were times I would totally shut down his advice because he didn't get the wisdom of the Lord about a situation like I thought he should. He may have gotten it by reading a book, and I would think he needs to get it out of prayer and time spent with God.

He would not take my advice because I was not "knowledgeable" enough on the subject like he was; even though I heard the Lord say to me a phrase or direction to go or not go, I was dismissed. Frustrating, right? You better believe it.

At the end of the day, in most situations, we realized we should've listened to one another and we were both right. Unity and diversity—it's a picture of the body of Christ.

I used to think you had to be in the secret place with the Lord for an allotted amount of time before you made any big decision, but the truth is, He can speak whenever and however He wants to. He can speak to you through a random book you are reading or a billboard on the side of the road, an advertisement on the side of a car on the highway, the Bible, through a person, or a still, small voice in your head. He speaks in all kinds of ways, and if we are paying attention, we will hear Him. We don't always have to fast and pray to hear God's voice. It's okay. At the same time, it's always a good idea to spend time in His presence.

Oftentimes, we make hearing God so complicated and religious when all we have to do is become aware of His voice at any time of day. It's so easy.

The main thing I want you to learn in this chapter is to respect the voice of God through others who do not look like you, talk like you, or walk like you in the Lord. If you cannot allow yourself to listen and consider the advice of someone else because you think they are not as spiritual as you, you will lack understanding, wisdom, knowledge, and direction, and eventually, you will look like a fool. You will miss assignments and direction because you refused to hear how God was speaking to you. And the influence and favor you carry will be limited.

Drawing from both kingly and priestly expands your field of favor, not to mention the untapped spheres of influence just waiting for you to display the glory of God. When you have both sides of the coin, so to speak, everything about you increases. You are not just a half of a coin, you are a full measure of its worth. Applying strategy with presence and presence with strategy opens up a whole new world of flowing in the prophetic to call God's will into existence, as well. Your vision for city transformation becomes possible.

God does nothing on the earth unless He reveals His secrets to His servants the prophets. (Amos 3:7)

So, back to how Jim and I worked this priest/king thing out. I decided to stop being so stubborn and fighting for my right to be right all the time. The more I listened to how Jim connected to God and the more he listened to how I connected to God, we started gleaning from one another, honoring one another, and using our strengths together.

One of us was not "more right" than the other, and we are BETTER TOGETHER than we are apart. We are more powerful together than we are apart. Because we were both willing to learn and respect how one another is wired, Jim has influenced me to be a priestly king, and I have influenced him to be a kingly priest.

Not only that, but I felt this was a new place of maturity God wanted to bring us into—to operate in both the kingly and the priestly. I became more than just priestly; I was now a priestly king! I feel like I carry *more* now: more depth, more honor for people, more respect for others different than me. Therefore, I am able to keep expanding, growing, and loving better.

As I said before, I needed to stop fighting for my right to be right and LISTEN to the other person so that I could GROW up. How are you doing with this concept?

All of us are bent a little one way more than the other and that's okay; the important thing is that both sides are awake, yielding to God and God's voice through others, and also learning from those voices. Do not just write it off as you are "not wired that way" and leave it to someone else to figure out. You are wired both ways, so lean into learning a new skill.

When operating as a kingly priest or a priestly king, you are moving into your story on earth that God planned before you were born. I believe this is part of maturing to walk in all the fullness that was put in you the day you decided to live for Jesus.

> *"And to the one who has made us to rule as a kingly priesthood to serve his God and Father—to him be glory and dominion throughout the eternity of eternities! Amen!" (Revelation 1:6 TPT)*

REVELATORY ENCOUNTER 10

Listen to my walk-through of this encounter at:
www.GloryOnDisplay.com

Set aside 15-25 minutes to encounter God in a fresh way that will bring you into a deeper revelation of being a kingly priest or a priestly king.

Have your journal ready to write down everything you see and hear so that you will remember and be a good steward (or you can write it here on this page).

Prayer to Partner with:

Holy Spirit, thank You for making me just the way I am. Thank You for putting me around others who will help me grow in both kingly and priestly anointing. I trust You to complete everything You started inside of me. I partner with You now as You reveal everything You want me to know.

Let's read a list (though not an *exhaustive* list) of the tendencies in the priestly category and tendencies in the kingly.

Circle all that you are most drawn to.

If you do not have a hard copy, make a note in your

journal of what words you are most drawn to in each category of the priestly and kingly.

Priestly

Intimacy with Jesus, intercession, angelic, prophecy, healing, evangelism, raising the dead, changing the atmosphere, soaking, time in His presence, dancing before the Lord in worship.

The priests open the gate between heaven and earth for the kings to do their part.

Kingly

Defend, protect, conquer, build, administer, and advance, to take territory so that what the devil has possession of is taken back and heaven invades earth in that part of their sphere of influence, resources, plans, strategies, and goals.

Kings have affluence and influence within a sphere of authority.

Ask Holy Spirit

Are my actions bent toward a king or a priest?

_____
_____
_____
_____

_____
_____

What do I need to know, Holy Spirit, about how I am wired (kingly/priestly)?

_____
_____
_____
_____
_____
_____

Highlight a close friend to me (or spouse if married). Are they more kingly or more priestly? How can I honor that anointing better? Have I been fighting for my right to be right in any of my relationships? If so, which relationship and what do You want me to do about that?

_____
_____
_____
_____
_____
_____

Going a Little Deeper

Write down what He says or shows you after each question.

Now, with your eyes closed, invite the Lord to have His way. Quiet yourself and breathe Him in, allowing every other thought or weight to melt away as you breathe out. Step into His realm, His reality. Find His eyes in that space and give Him a big hug. Love on Him. He has been waiting for you and is very glad to see you and meet with you.

Lord, are there any hindrances in the way that are keeping me from moving into both kingly and priestly anointings? If so, what are they?

_____
_____
_____
_____
_____
_____

Lord, are there any boundaries or walls I put up regarding this area of kingly or priestly? If so, please show me what the wall or boundary looks like and what the name of it is.

_____
_____
_____
_____
_____
_____

God's Glory on Display

Lord, please remove any walls, boundaries, or hindrances that have held me back from stepping into this area of kingly/priestly in my life.

_____
_____
_____
_____
_____

Now allow the Lord to give you a picture of Him breaking down any walls, boundaries, or hindrances. Write down what He did and how He did it.

_____
_____
_____
_____
_____

We do not need our own walls or things to hide behind because Scripture tells us,

> *The name of the LORD is a fortified tower; the righteous run to it and are safe. (Proverbs 18:10)*

Now, pray in the Spirit, thanking Him for what He has done. When a boundary we put in place is removed by God, there is one less thing in between the intimacy of you and Him. As you thank Him, joy will come in like a flood.

II

THE LIVING WATER

The Hostile Takeover

For those who do not know, I grew up in a Christian home under a set of parents who loved and adored me (probably more than my other sisters... I'm kidding. The youngest can say things like this). I asked Jesus to come into my heart at four years old and encountered a baptism of the Spirit and spoke in tongues in my teenage years. My parents are lovers of Jesus, intercessors, very prophetic, full of the Holy Spirit, and full of biblical knowledge, understanding, wisdom, and experience.

I remember being woken up as a teenager late at night as they had groups of people over and prayer time started. There was a lot of deliverance, healing, and speaking in tongues! All that to say, I was exposed to it all and then some. It would probably offend some of you if I went on telling you some of the things I saw

God do. I have seen what the power of the Holy Spirit can do and I welcome it.

> *He that believeth on me, as the scripture hath said, out of his belly shall flow rivers of living water. (John 7:38)*

As I said before, I had experienced a level of the Holy Spirit before, but the first time I really experienced Living Water flowing from my belly, in almost a hostile takeover way, was when I went on a women's retreat my mom was putting on a few years ago. Most of the attendees were not as exposed to this kind of wildness of the Spirit, so I was trying to keep myself and the Spirit tame so as to not scare them or put them off.

I had already spoken at one of the sessions, and I was pretty sure I broke some people by accident as I tend to go straight to the deep places and chase barriers out of the room. I feel like life is not worth living if people don't get cracked open and set free.

So, I am at this women's retreat, and at the night session during worship, someone gives a word about how "God is as close as the air you breathe; His glory is right here." As soon as she said those words, I began to feel something jumping in my tummy. It felt like the Holy Spirit in my belly was about to come up and out. I told everyone, in a calm manner of course, "I think we are supposed to take a minute and partner with this word. Everyone, pray in your heavenly language, and if you have never spoken in this language, it's a good time to activate it, or you can just start worshiping Him in your own words!"

I began to speak in tongues, louder and louder and louder. I knew the Holy Spirit was knocking on the door, "Do I have permission to go?" and of course, my answer was "Yes!" I immediately felt like someone was pushing on my stomach and I began to make this "whoa, whoa, whoa, whoa, whoa" noise. I couldn't control it because I gave Him control, so I was laughing in between "whoas."

My mom had been having heart rhythm problems that year. As I am practically convulsing and making this sound and laughing—oh, and apologizing because I knew I was probably freaking someone out—I see in the spirit a heavenly defibrillator an angel was putting on my mom's chest. So I made my way over to her while still making this ridiculous sound and I lay my hands on her. I tell her there is a defibrillator from heaven on her chest and God is healing her heart.

The Spirit now hits her and she is expressing a "whoa" in between my "whoas." I was crying and laughing so hard—and apologizing. This went on for several minutes until I finally got on the floor and crawled away from her.

She was totally healed for months after that! I had never experienced that kind of bubbling from the Living River, Holy Spirit in my life. It was a hostile takeover, indeed.

I realized later that the sound I was making mimicked the defibrillator, or rather someone getting shocked by the defibrillator. Holy Spirit is so fun, isn't He? Adventure is always waiting; we just have to be willing to let Him run!

What is the Living Water?

Jesus answered, "Everyone who drinks this water will be thirsty again, but whoever drinks the water I give them will never thirst. Indeed, the water I give them will become in them a spring of water welling up to eternal life." The woman said to him, "Sir, give me this water so that I won't get thirsty and have to keep coming here to draw water." (John 4:13-15)

The other night, I had a group over to my house. We were talking about being overtaken by the Holy Spirit and how the Spirit is that living water inside us that we can access at any moment, like a well you can draw from that is alive. One of the people in the group started sharing how they always wondered why they never saw or felt like there was actually a well of Living Water inside of them. They said they had never pictured the Lord in that way, but Holy Spirit was starting to help them see.

I began to tell the story of when Holy Spirit took me over at the retreat and it was like a gushing coming from my tummy, like a geyser of water. This also speaks of the place of the womb, where we dwell in Christ. It is our inner-man area where a new reality is set as we spend time in the inner-inner chambers with the Lord. The belly is where new things are birthed and protected, grown, and strengthened.

When the Holy Spirit took me over, I gave Him permission to do so. He will never do anything you are not willing to allow Him to do, but you better believe it will be memorable!

I thought about what my friend had said and what I should've said, which is, "It isn't literally water, so no need to focus on water itself. It is an analogy Jesus uses to talk about the Holy Spirit." But then I began to meditate on the other verses in the Bible.

> *"Come," says the Holy Spirit and the Bride in divine duet. Let everyone who hears this duet join them in saying, "Come." Let everyone gripped with spiritual thirst say, "Come." And let everyone who craves the gift of living water come and drink it freely. "Come." (Revelation 22:17 TPT)*

> *Then on the most important day of the feast, the last day, Jesus stood and shouted out to the crowds—"All you thirsty ones, come to me! Come to me and drink! Believe in me so that rivers of living water will burst out from within you, flowing from your innermost being, just like the Scripture says!" (John 7:37-38 TPT)*

A few days went by and in the morning, I started reading John 4. No particular reason other than I wanted a refresher on the book of John. And of course, I read the story of when Jesus met the woman at the well. I took notice that the Lord may be trying to speak to me. Go figure.

I thought to myself, "Do I even know what the Living Water is? I had always just assumed it was the Holy Spirit." So, I asked the Lord, "What is the Living Water exactly?" As I pressed in a little deeper with an ear toward the Spirit and curiosity, it began to unfold.

Getting ready to write some thoughts down about it all, my personal journal was opened up to a specific page—on its own. It was a page at the beginning of my journal. I start to read what I wrote on the page, thinking I must've left it open to remind myself of something.

It was a dream I had called, *The Waterfall Cabin*. I realized this was God that made this happen and this dream was the answer to my question.

In the dream, I was at a campground waiting to hear Joyce Meyer speak. I was in a small cabin and others were arriving to join in the session. As we were waiting for Joyce, a woman came in and sat down. She said, "I am going to put this container on the desk to catch water, because the last time I did this, it rained."

I was thinking, "What?!" She began to play her keyboard, a weird series of sounds. I was squirming a bit, not wanting to dishonor Holy Spirit by her trying to get Him to do tricks for us, like raining into a bowl. The next thing I know, my mom is next to me and we are both lying on the floor. My mom put a small metal bowl near my head to catch the rain when it came. I felt more at ease knowing she thought it was okay (your mother often represents Holy Spirit in your dreams). I then start to hear drops of water pinging the metal bowl and other people's containers, as well. I then saw water running down the walls! I looked in our metal bowl and there was water in it. Oddly enough, the floors were all dry. It had only rained inside the containers.

Revelation started flowing in as I re-read this dream. Maybe I was just slow the first time I had this dream, but I realized we are the container for the Lord. Jesus is the source of the LIVING WATER. He is LIFE itself. Without Him, we are dead. But with Him, we are alive! We will spend the rest of our days here on earth and in heaven communing with the Father of lights in all of His fullness.

The Spirit of the LORD shall rest upon him, the Spirit of wisdom and understanding, the Spirit of counsel and might, the Spirit of knowledge and of the fear of the LORD, and He will delight in the fear of the Lord. (Isaiah 11:2-3)

This verse describes the Holy Spirit coming on Jesus. When Jesus ascended into heaven after He rose from the dead, He sent His Spirit—the very Spirit of God—to live inside of US so that we could be in union with Him! When we open ourselves (containers) up to the rain of the Lord, the LIFE of the Lord, the sound of Lord, the voice of the Lord, the ways of Lord, we are allowing God's presence to invade our minds and bodies so that we can access every single thing we need to live on the earth and manifest heaven here and now. This allows His Love-Kingdom to be known and shown. Not just for a day, but for a lifetime. Every single day, minute, and second we are made to manifest His goodness. This is the water that all men are thirsty for: Jesus.

The Living Water *is* the Spirit of God, but the source is Jesus, who is the fullness of everything. Holy Spirit was sent as a seal that we belong to Jesus through His blood shed and forgiveness once and for all. He is the answer to every situation. His Spirit living inside of us gives us access to everything Jesus! Our job is to set out our containers and receive the Living Water, however it may come, and everyone around us gets the benefit of meeting and encountering the King.

Remember I was there to hear Joyce Meyer in my dream? Guess what her name means? According to Wikipedia, it was first from the French deriving from the Latin meaning "Lord." Hilarious, right? I was there to meet and hear the "Lord."

Another obvious meaning of Joyce is "rejoice." My name book gives the spiritual connotation and inherent meaning (from the English in this case) of a name along with a Bible verse. This is what *The Name Book* by Dorothy Astoria says:

Joyce: "Vivacious" and "Gift of God."

You will show me the path of LIFE; IN YOUR PRESENCE is FULLNESS of joy; at your RIGHT HAND are pleasures forevermore. (Psalm 16:11 NKJV)

Who is LIFE? Jesus.

Who is the FULLNESS as we come in the presence of God? Jesus.

Who is at the RIGHT HAND of God? Jesus.

It all comes back to Jesus. This is who we take our drink from.

The Intentional Sound

As the girl played a sound (in my dream) on her instrument, it accessed a flow of the Living Water of heaven. What is the sound you are playing? We all have a sound. When we speak, vibrations run throughout our body to the air around us and move and shape things. When you hear a deep bass sound while listening to a song, it vibrates your chest, right? Sound is moving your molecules, bringing change.

This is what you do to people when you release the sound of heaven. It is not a matter of, *Am I releasing something?* It is a matter of, *hat and who am I releasing?* When you operate in your gifts, you are aligning with the sound of heaven and releasing Living Water to thirsty people around you. You are quenching a never-ending thirst they have been longing for. Jesus is the thirst quencher and you are the container that holds Him.

Our movements make a sound, as well. Our dance, our walk, our run, our wave...it all makes a sound. The intentionality to hear heaven, to hear the voice of God inside of you, is what will bring heaven to earth. It is what will bring the fullness of Christ through the Holy Spirit into atmospheres around you. As you allow Holy Spirit to bubble from your innermost being, a sound will appear that changes and rearranges the course of history.

Turn your attention to the Holy One to hear what He is saying and doing as you release your sound of heaven in any room you are in. Allow the Holy Spirit to overtake your spirit-man in such a way that you are no longer controlling, but yielding to Holy Spirit, the God of the universe, to be in control.

The Lord will guide you continually,
giving you water when you are dry
and restoring your strength.
You will be like a well-watered garden,
like an ever-flowing spring. (Isaiah 58:11 NLT)

The source of the Living Water is Jesus. God, Jesus, and Holy Spirit are three in one. When you are baptized in the Spirit, you are filled with the power of the Spirit, the power of God Himself. We can access this water at any time and where the river flows, everything will live and produce fruit.

Fruit trees of all kinds will grow on both banks of the river. Their leaves will not wither, nor will their fruit fail. Every month they will bear fruit, because the water from the sanctuary flows to them. Their fruit will serve for food and their leaves for healing. (Ezekiel 47:12)

REVELATORY ENCOUNTER 11

Listen to my walk-through of this encounter at:
www.GloryOnDisplay.com

Grab your journal for this final encounter. It's gonna be good.

Today, we are going to practice setting our bowls out to collect the rain of the Holy Spirit.

You are the bowl being set out to encounter the drink of the Lord.

He will bring a refreshing to you as you sit in His presence.

It is the ultimate refreshing sensation.

Think upon His goodness.

Right now, Holy Spirit is flashing up moments in time when you have seen His goodness in your life. With each memory flash, thank Him, praise Him, adore Him.

Lord, thank You for Your never-ending mercy and love in my life.
I am a container for Your glory, the very essence of You.
I set myself in front of You as a container to receive Your rain.

Open yourself up (however that looks for you) and listen for the sounds of heaven.

Now, move the sounds you hear out of your mouth into the atmosphere, creating an atmosphere for Him to fill.

The atmosphere you are creating is not foreign to you; it is home.

This is your place of shelter.

This is a place of rest and renewal; of oil and wine; healing and power.

You have made an atmosphere now like a bowl set out for Holy Spirit to rain in.

Now, receive His rain on your face and into your being with your eyes closed and behold Him.

If you want to keep going further, ask the Lord where else He wants to take you and why.

He's ALWAYS ready for an adventure!

Just don't forget to write it down!

Homework Every Day This Week

In a quiet and unrushed place, read these verses with the Holy Spirit as a declaration over your life and the lives that you touch.

> [23] *"Be glad, O children of Zion,*
> *and rejoice in the Lord your God,*
> *for he has given the early rain for your vindication;*
> *he has poured down for you abundant rain,*
> *the early and the latter rain, as before.*

²⁴ "The threshing floors shall be full of grain;
  the vats shall overflow with wine and oil.
²⁵ I will restore to you the years
  that the swarming locust has eaten,
the hopper, the destroyer, and the cutter,
  my great army, which I sent among you.

²⁶ "You shall eat in plenty and be satisfied,
  and praise the name of the Lord your God,
  who has dealt wondrously with you.
And my people shall never again be put to shame.
²⁷ You shall know that I am in the midst of Israel,
  and that I am the Lord your God and there is
none else.
And my people shall never again be put to shame.

²⁸ "And it shall come to pass afterward,
  that I will pour out my Spirit on all flesh;
your sons and your daughters shall prophesy,
  your old men shall dream dreams,
  and your young men shall see visions.
²⁹ Even on the male and female servants
  in those days I will pour out my Spirit."
(Joel 2:23-29 ESV)

MARY BAKER and her husband, Jim, have 3 boys and are the Senior Leaders of Zion Christian Fellowship in Powell, Ohio. The church is marked by worship, a strong presence of God, healings, miracles, several dead raisings and a passion for personal and regional transformation. Mary also serves as the Worship Arts Pastor and is known for leading people to experience His presence in worship where healing, joy, freedom, and deliverance are common in this environment. She has written many worship songs and has released three solo worship albums, the latest is The Way You Move Me. In addition, she wrote a collaboration of "Prophetic War Songs for the Bride" with another artist called And The Walls Came Down. Her desire is to raise up the Bride of Christ through training & equipping, release her sound to change atmospheres, bring people into encounters with Jesus and manifest heavenly realities wherever she is.

www.ingramcontent.com/pod-product-compliance
Lightning Source LLC
Chambersburg PA
CBHW060320050426
42449CB00011B/2570